Helen Murray

was born in Belfast and studied drama in London before pursuing a career
in journalism. She began reporting for the *Irish News* in 1998
and then moved to Dublin in 2000 where she has since been working for
The Sunday Tribune. In 2004 she was appointed features editor of
The Sunday Tribune's iMagazine.

Tanya Ling

is an artist who trained as a fashion designer at Central Saint Martin's School
of Art in London. She is well-known as an award-winning fashion illustrator
who has worked for many of the world's leading fashion titles, including
Vogue and *Harper's Bazaar*. Among others, she has illustrated for Jil Sander,
Louis Vuitton and Diane Von Furstenberg. Tanya lives and works in London.
See www.tanyaling.com

What Lies Beneath

What Lies Beneath

HELEN MURRAY

Illustrations by Tanya Ling

ᘉERCIER PRESS

MERCIER PRESS
Douglas Village, Cork
Website: www.mercierpress.ie

Trade enquiries to CMD Distribution
55A Spruce Avenue, Stillorgan Industrial Park
Blackrock, County Dublin
Tel: (01) 294 2560; Fax: (01) 294 2564
E-mail: cmd@columba.ie

ISBN 1 85635 477 6
10 9 8 7 6 5 4 3 2 1

A CIP record for this title is available
from the British Library

Mercier Press receives financial assistance from
the Arts Council/An Chomhairle Ealaíon

Printed in Ireland by ColourBooks Ltd

Contents

Dedication

For the woman who

bought my first set of underwear,

my mother, Elizabeth Marie Murray

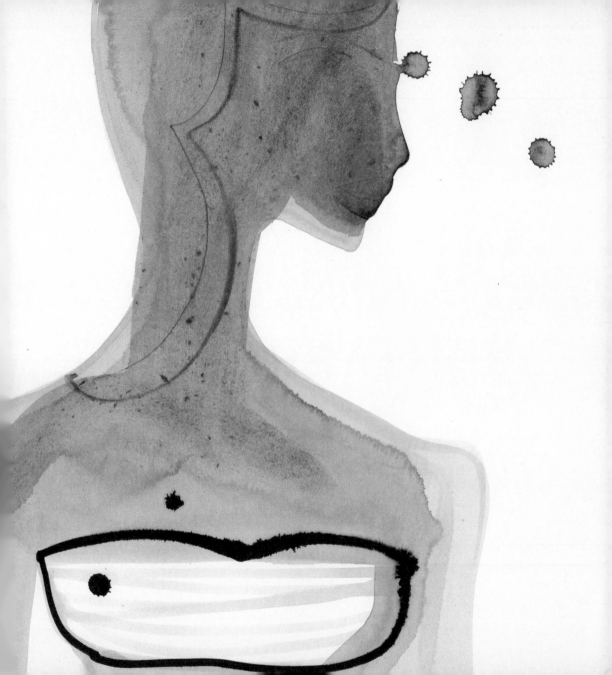

Introduction

Just as clothing is an expression of the person underneath, underwear can also reflect the style and the personality of the woman wearing it. If you want to get to know a woman, have a peek in her drawers, the contents might just tell you more than she will.

You can tell a lot about a woman from her underwear. Not only does it betray her size and shape, it will also provide an insight into her personality and age, and may even shed some light on her plans for later that evening.

Women's underwear, or lingerie, as it has become known, has undergone a series of metamorphoses during the last one hundred years as has the position of women in society. Women have won the right to vote and climbed to positions of power and influence unimaginable to their corset-bound ancestors. Similarly, from whalebone to Wonderbra, underwear has been transformed from cumbersome size-reducing apparatus to garments designed for support, seduction and even comfort.

What brought about such a dramatic change in the contents of a woman's underwear drawer? Was it independence or fashion? Where there were once knee-length knickers there is now a diamanté-studded thong. Similarly, breasts that were strapped and flattened by bust-bodices are now rounded and firmed in padded bras.

What Lies Beneath takes a look at underwear fashion during the twentieth century and explores the effect society and culture has had upon a woman's first layer of clothing.

This book is not simply a historical examination of underwear. Instead I have chosen to look at underwear through the lenses of Shape, Fashion, Politics and Culture, which by their nature are not mutually exclusive. Therefore though references to important historical developments recur, each chapter can be read separately or as part of an interrelated whole.

The women's movement has been documented by historians and captured in literature and art but we have yet to look under the skirts of the women who brought about this revolution to discover the changes, if any, that lurk beneath.

"If clothes maketh the man, then surely underwear maketh the woman."

Chapter One
Shape

In the absence of our underwear, what shape are we in? Mostly, very different. If the clothes maketh the man, then surely underwear maketh the woman. From the corset to the Wonderbra, women's underwear has changed the physical form in varying degrees. One hundred years ago a woman simply could not close the fastenings on her dress without being cinched into her corset. A woman's underwear was an essential instrument for creating the shape that society expected and fashion dictated.

Today's woman might not look so noticeably different without her underwear but you can guarantee that without her bra her breasts would not be so firm. If she is a devotee of the more substantial elasticated knicker her stomach wouldn't be quite so smooth, her bottom not so rounded.

The corset is probably the most controversial garment ever worn by women. It has been demonised and glorified, castigated as a symbol of a woman's repression and yet determinedly worn in various forms for centuries. Similarly, contemporary underwear has been the subject of criticism from feminists such as Germaine Greer and the late Andrea Dworkin, both of whom urged women to discard their bras and refuse to conform to society's idealised image of the feminine figure.

From the Rational Dress movement at the turn of the twentieth century right up to the second wave of feminism in the 1970s, women have been repeatedly told that their corsets and brassieres are nothing more than the trappings of a patriarchal society. But despite the 'lingerie lectures' strong independent women all over the world continue to wear and sometimes even flaunt their underwear. They buy it for themselves and they give it to each other as gifts, which raises the question – are we all misguided? Fashion and feminism have always been at odds but what about the woman in between?

Corset Controversy

At the turn of the twentieth century, the fashionable shape of the day was captured by illustrator and author, Charles Dana Gibson. He created the Gibson Girl, the all-American young woman whose style and figure dominated fashion magazines across Europe and the United States. Her S-bend shape was often reproduced wearing fashionable shirt-waists that emphasised her long, sloping bust, flat front and grace-fully curved hips. With her hair piled loosely on top of her head, the Gibson Girl was seen as the embodiment of the modern young woman.

This shape was impossible to achieve without the assistance of the corset. As the first decade of the twentieth century advanced, a long body and narrow hips became the fashion, so much so that for a brief period the fashionable lady's corset descended almost halfway down the thigh.

The pros and cons of corset-wearing have been heavily debated and Valerie Steele recounts much of this in her book, *The Corset, A Cultural History*. She makes reference to the numerous articles published in health journals – almost always written by men – which detailed the grave risks associated with tight-lacing.

Steele quotes from an article published in the British medical periodical, *The Lancet,* in 1868, which stated unequivocally that tight-lacing seriously limited, and in some cases prevented, the respiratory movements of the diaphragm.

Although more recent medical research has confirmed that restricting the chest does inhibit breathing, Steele argues it was unlikely that corset-wearing led to permanent ill-health but was rather a contributory factor to faint- ing for women engaged in physically-exerting activities such as dancing. Her examination of corsets from this period has revealed that they were often designed to be undone swiftly should the wearer find herself extremely short of breath.

> **the corset is probably the most controversial garment ever to be worn by women**

Steele argues that nineteenth-century women did not reduce their waists by inches to achieve a shape unrecognisable from their own and says the notion that women have been oppressed by a capitalist-fuelled fashion system ignores the fact that adornment and self-fashioning long preceded the rise of capitalism. She con- sidered it rather short-sighted to condemn the corset as an instrument of torture or the women encased in it as victims, enslaved to fashion by their foolish vanity.

But women's bodies were reduced and moulded into a shape that was a far cry from their natural figures. To be made smaller, narrower and slighter than a man has always been, and continues to be, a sign of femininity. In the January 1900 edition of *Lady of the House*, a magazine circulated throughout Ireland and the UK, 'Thompson Corsets' advertised their underwear which was available in a number of Dublin shops:

These world-renowned Corsets have been entirely
Remodelled, and are now the Perfection of Shape,
and meet the prevailing fashion of long-waist.
The most comfortable and durable corset made
And therefore the cheapest.

Accompanying the text is a small illustration of a curvaceous young woman wearing her corset and gazing serenely upwards. Individual words were selected by the advertisers to be singled out with capital letters; 'Perfection of Shape' is particularly arresting to the eye and appears almost as a promise to the potential buyer.

This advertisement appeared in most editions of *Lady of the House* magazine in the early years of the twentieth century. Ten years later, in January 1910, in between the 'Women's Parliament' – a debating forum (which that week gave particular consideration to the pros and cons of early-rising) – and 'At What Age Should Girls "Come Out"?', McBirney & Co. on Aston Quay, Dublin, advertised their French corsets, also guaranteed to provide the 'Perfect Shape'.

It is apparent that 'Perfect Shape' was not the female form Mother Nature intended but something that could and ought to be purchased. It was a metamorphosis. As Thompson Corsets clearly stated, their designs had recently been remodelled to provide the most fashionable silhouette. Women were reminded of the imperfection of their natural physique and that the precise nature of their ideal or even 'Perfect' shape was subject to the whimsical turn of fashion.

Perhaps the women reading *Lady of the House* did not seriously view this form of advertising as a direct criticism of their bodies. The accompanying illustrations were invariably small and discreetly located at the lower corner of the advert, unlike the advertisements of today where the image is the single most important element.

Men and children also wore various forms of corsets up until the turn of the twentieth century, although they were not as restrictive as those worn by fashionable women. Well-to-do gentlemen wore belt-like girdles around their waists to make their chests appear broader and it was believed that bodices improved the posture and deportment of children.

All of this is important to remember when considering the corset in the context of women's position in society: it was not only the female body that was subject to such physical restriction. Bodies in general were believed to be in need of support but it was only women who were criticised and warned of the ill-effects of wearing their underwear. Not only were they persuaded by fashion into the tightest stays, or supports, but they were also admonished for their vanity.

Although women were encouraged to transform their bodies, dramatic reduction in size – or 'tight-lacing' as it was known – was considered unladylike and vulgar. In the 'World of Dress' section of *Lady of the House*, the writer criticised the woman who dared to tie her stays too close for comfort:

It is strange to notice the attraction that anything tight has for the stout woman. Her stays are always drawn tighter than anyone else's. She wears tightly-fitting garments — so tight that she presents the appearance vulgarly known as 'looking as if she was melted and poured into them,' and to crown it all, her skirts are always short.

Underwear soon began to be adapted in accordance with a woman's activities. At the turn of the twentieth century, as women were just a few years away from the vote, not only were their underclothes providing the essential shape, they were also designed to facilitate movement. As the popularity of sporting activities among Victorian women increased, advertisers used this to attract buyers by christening their garments names like 'Ball's Riding Corset' and 'W. B. America's leading Cyclist Corset'.

The Corset is Dead!

In 1912, from his lofty position as one of the most daring couturiers in Paris, Paul Poiret decreed that the corset was dead. In the subsequent years he never failed to congratulate himself for his role in taking the first generation of twentieth-century women out of their corsets. His modern reinterpretation of the eighteenth-century Directoire period, characterised by empire-line high-waists and long flowing skirts, was thought to be more liberating than contemporary Edwardian fashions. (Despite his dramatic pronouncement, Poiret designed the 'hobble skirt' a few years later. He may have liberated a woman's torso from stays but he merely transferred the restriction from their chests to their legs.)

There was a seismic shift in what was considered to be the fashionable shape during the 1920s. Instead of the previous variations upon the hourglass figure, the ideal shape became narrow and straight-hipped. Skirts were raised higher than they had ever been before and ankles and calves were on display. This sudden exposure of areas previously swathed in skirts and petticoats, transferred the focus from the waist and hips to the arms and legs.

Women had become more independent during this period as a result of increased employment and attaining the vote. Perhaps as a reflection of this recent access to privileges previously held by men only, their clothes began to look boyish. 'Ganymede' was the nickname given to the style of the 1920s flapper, named after the Shakespearean heroine who dressed herself as a boy so she could seek her fortune independently from her family.

> " the fashionable figure bore more resemblance to the male physique "

Women's clothes were simplified, layers of petticoats were discarded and everyday dress had a capacity for movement as never before. The thoroughly modern woman cut her hair and flattened her chest, the waistline was dropped to the hip and skirts became straighter. Legs and arms could swing in their sockets and sportswear, pioneered by designers like Coco Chanel, brought a new lease of life to fashion.

More significantly, despite these dramatic changes in fashion, the supposed ideal shape was no longer brought about by underwear alone but was expected to be controlled by the woman herself. Fashion magazines like *Vogue* began to feature articles on weight-loss and exercises designed to slim the torso which prompted one writer to ask in 1922:

> With the aid of the corsetiere, the physical culturist and the non-starchy diet, shall we soon develop a race of slender, willowy women?

The fashionable figure bore more resemblance to the male physique or in fact a pre-pubescent boy than anything in the history of women's dress. The unrealistic silhouette seems like a bitter pill to swallow given the advancement of women's rights during this time. Although strengthened by parliaments and pay packets, they were weakened by their slight frames. Even women courageous enough to endure imprisonment in their struggle for equality opted to shrink their stature as a means of highlighting their cause. Only a few years before, Irish feminist Hannah Sheehy-Skeffington had chosen to starve herself as a means of raising awareness of Irishwomen's suffrage. Fired up by reports of the hunger-strikes of her English counterparts, Sheehy-Skeffington and a number of Irish suffragettes refused food during their period of imprisonment in Mountjoy jail. They used the gradual weakening of their bodies as a means to engender public support for their cause.

The Return of Glamour

Hollywood and the movie industry had become the purveyors of style and glamour by the 1930s following the introduction of 'talkies' – the nickname given to movies with sound. In the years following the Wall Street Crash of 1929, the movie theatre provided a much-needed antidote to the drab existence of men and women across America and all over the world.

The gamine look of the 1920s was replaced by an ultra-feminine glamour as the fashion world and Hollywood cast aside the fragile boy-girl look in favour of a more curvaceous silhouette. In addition to rediscovering the waist and the voluptuous bosom, the shoulders of evening dresses and coats were padded, giving women a breadth across the body previously only encouraged among men. This almost triangular silhouette, which faded into the narrow waists and skirts below, created a warrior-like shape, a far-cry from the fragile form which had dominated fashion during the previous decade.

Designers began cutting cloth on the bias – a technique previously only used in lingerie – so that it draped close to the body. As clothing became more fitted, the figure underneath became harder to disguise and, once again, lingerie was designed to coerce the body into the desired shape. Although the look was considered more feminine and arguably more possible for women to emulate than the androgynous look of the 1920s, the shape could only be created by wearing the appropriate undergarments.

Mae West, the star of movie classics such as *Destry Rides Again* and *The Blue Angel* was one of the most celebrated Hollywood stars of the era and an ardent fan of brassieres and 'foundation' wear.

Maria Riva wrote in her biography of her mother, Marlene Dietrich, published in 1992, that Dietrich often admitted to having 'ugly breasts' and, in order to disguise her unsatisfactory bosom, she spent vast amounts of time and money searching for the perfect bra.

Dietrich owned every type of brassiere on the market and, according to her daughter, often required endless underwear fittings when putting together an outfit. Each ensemble demanded specific lingerie and would be individually packaged and labelled accordingly. Dietrich never gave up her search for the ultimate brassiere and upon arriving in any new town or city would unfailingly hunt down the lingerie boutique in the hope that they might be the purveyors of her holy grail. Riva writes that when her underwear failed to deliver the effect Dietrich was determined to achieve, the brassiere would be cast aside in disgust and wide strips of adhesive would be employed to create the uplifted look she so desired.

> " Dietrich often admitted to having 'ugly breasts' "

Seventy years later and what's changed? Today adhesive strips, or 'tit tape' as it has become known, are often employed by women to enhance their chests and guard against total exposure when wearing more revealing items of clothing. It would seem that fashion and underwear designers are still not communicating on the subject of women and their real bodies.

In 1935 the American underwear giant Warner Brothers came to the earth-shattering conclusion that women's bodies were in fact not all the same and introduced cup sizing. They concluded that not only were women different sizes but they were also different shapes. They devised the 'Alphabet Bra' which had four sizes – A, B, C and D. Previously, manufacturers had produced bras in junior, medium, full and, least flattering of all, 'full with wide waist'.

During the Second World War, the fashion world was forced to plant two feet firmly on the ground. There was little time or money to dedicate to the excess and frivolity of high fashion and couture. Rationing and shortages influenced the shape of women more so than any magazine picture or Hollywood starlet. In the UK, the government had introduced restrictions covering the design and construction of clothes from socks to underpants; all garments made according to these regulations were stamped with a 'Utility' label. The Victoria and Albert Museum in London has a number of Utility girdles among its costume collection which were sold in British department stores during and after the war.

One piece in particular, a 1940s Marks and Spencer 'roll-on' corset, carried a label 'to fit waist of 25 inches' but yet when the waist of the garment was measured the circumference came to just 18 inches. This peach-coloured corset with suspender clasps attached is stiff to the touch and, although elastic, has little give in the fabric. The shape such a garment provided – a waist reduction of 7 inches – was a far cry from the owner's natural form. Such a garment must have been a struggle to squeeze into and was undoubtedly a relief to remove at the end of each day.

More women were working than ever before as a result of the war effort and it is generally accepted that they revelled in their new-found productivity. However, such a restrictive undergarment as held by the Victoria and Albert Museum would indicate that these women traversed new industrial territories while firmly encased by their underwear.

A New Look for Ladies

Following the privations and grief of the Second World War, the fashion world was only too eager to distance itself from the sombre, thrifty lines of the 1940s and to embrace a new style. Christian Dior's Carolle line in 1947 turned the tide of fashion with wide and expansive skirts set off by narrow waists and pointed chests.

Although much emphasis was placed upon the nipped-in waists of this period, equal consideration was given to breasts. Manufacturers who previously focused on transforming the waist and torso turned their attention towards the all-important bosom.

Once again Hollywood led the way in promoting the hourglass figure and actress Lana Turner became known as 'the Sweater Girl' — she earned her nickname not so much for her close-fitting woollens as for her curves underneath. Turner and many actresses of the period wore bras that lifted their breasts and, just as importantly, separated them into two very distinct cone-shaped peaks. Such a look could only be achieved with expert engineering and underwear designers began producing bras that could lift and mould the slackest breast into a bosom that could poke your eye out.

But before 'the Sweater Girl' there was Jane Russell's cleavage — a vision of womanhood so voluptuous it was deemed too explicit for the silver screen. The movie featuring her first starring role, *The Outlaw*, was banned by the American Film Board until producer Howard Hughes agreed to cut several of her more daring scenes. The movie had caused such controversy and was so delayed by the film censors that by the time it was eventually released, the previously unknown Russell was the most celebrated pin-up of the day.

Hughes' most consuming passion, above movies and women, was aeroplanes, however this engineering prowess was not confined to the air. Upon seeing the first takes of Russell in action he announced to the film crew that they simply must 'make the most of Jane's breasts'.

Hughes utilised his engineering skills and set about designing a bra for Russell's substantial bosom to ensure that not only were her breasts lifted and brought together to showcase her cleavage but also so that they would appear rounded. The final structure is reported to have been a piece of engineering mastery but extremely uncomfortable. According to Hughes' biographers, Peter Harry Brown and Pat H. Broeske, Russell took one look at the 'pilot' version and dismissed it immediately as impossible to wear. To the consternation of the wardrobe mistress, she tossed aside the Hughes design and stuffed her own bra with tissue assuring those around her that the film-maker would never notice. Russell was proved correct and, after years of wrangling with the censors, Hughes finally unveiled his much-talked about movie in 1943. On the night of the world premiere Hughes proudly declared from the steps of the Hollywood movie theatre that 'Sex has not been rationed'.

Although the movie was not critically acclaimed, its success at the box-office ensured Jane Russell's cleavage was burned onto the consciousness of men and women across America. As for the aeronautical-designed bra, that particular blueprint remains with Howard Hughes.

The 1950s fashion demanded larger breasts and bra manufacturers were not slow to pick up on the demand. Scandale, a French company, launched what they believed to be a 'very secret' nylon brassiere with additional plastic cups that could be inflated by the wearer by blowing into a plastic pipette.

A woman's natural shape was of no concern to the fashion industry or lingerie manufacturers who thought only of how they might manipulate it. As in previous decades, the female figure was viewed as an incomplete article that ought to be moulded, cinched and lifted into the preferred shape: a tiny waist, a raised and pointed bosom and wide hips. The softness and sensuous aesthetic of the 1930s was gone and replaced by a more angular and structured form. Women appeared birdlike and fragile, their hourglass shape carefully honed and packaged, flesh tightly squeezed and coerced into a rigid silhouette – a body kept firmly under control by underwear.

Stick-thin and Sexed-up

The fashion world's idea of the desired figure had changed dramatically by the time the sexual revolution took hold during the 1960s and, while women were no longer encouraged to reduce the size of their waists and puff up their chests, they had effectively started to shrink.

Popular culture became obsessed by youth. The sexual revolution promoted an independent and responsibility-free existence and who better to carry this off than the young? Fashion hastened to reflect this mood and the womanly shape of the 1950s was replaced by a slender, boyish frame.

The Sweater Girls faded into the distance and in their place emerged stick-thin nymphs who peered out at the world from under thick black false-eyelashes and heavily kohl-rimmed eyes. The waist was no longer the focus, raised hemlines had created the mini-skirt and the mystique previously associated with the hips and thighs vanished overnight.

Underwear was simplified; petticoats, slips and the 'waspie' girdle – a prerequisite for the New Look – were considered outdated and the trappings of an older, stuffier generation. Similarly, mini-skirts put paid to stockings and suspenders while pantihose, or tights as they became known, were adopted into the mainstream wardrobe.

> ## The physical ideal was the androgynous waif

British designer Mary Quant pioneered the miniskirt along with her make-up and lingerie collection and, in 1966, when she was invited to Buckingham Palace to receive an OBE for her achievements, she famously wore a miniskirt measuring only 14 inches from waist to hem.

Quant's designs were the fashion embodiment of the 1960s and everything associated with 'cool London'. Instead of the Parisian catwalks, Mary Quant found inspiration on the streets and in the nightclubs of the capital city. Her vibrant make-up, short skirts and colourful tights seemed to express the desire for adventure and discovery felt by her own generation.

The Victoria and Albert Museum have a selection of underwear designed by Mary Quant. One set of brassiere and panties in her trademark 'barely brown' colour is decorated with her trademark flower motif. When compared with the Utility scheme girdles and corsets of the previous decade, her bra and knickers appear to provide significantly more movement, however, the fabric and structure of both pieces are surprisingly stiff to the touch. So although there were most definitely fewer layers, the notion of 'freedom' attached to her designs was entirely relative to the style of underwear in years gone by.

Although the physical ideal in this celebration of youth and sex was the androgynous waif, the reality, as always, was somewhat different. Mary Quant's underwear was directional and exceedingly influential but it was by no means available along every high street. Women were still purchasing their smalls from department stores and local boutiques where the skimpy separates had not yet caught on.

This period is perhaps the first example of when fashion and real women parted company.

The fashion world promoted a shape that most women had no hope of emulating: no matter how complicated or restrictive their underwear could be, it was never going to provide the stick-thin legs and arms on the pages of every magazine. Previously women could at least make an attempt at the overall fashionable shape; they may not have had the same vital statistics as Jane Russell or Marlene Dietrich but at least they could ensure they went in and out in roughly the same places. No sooner did fashion decree women should reveal more of their bodies, than the 'ideal' shape became an impossible dream for most women. This marked a significant shift in the purpose of underwear which had previously been worn and marketed as garments that made women look good in their clothes. At this point, women could no longer rely on their underwear for serious body sculpting. That discipline had to be imposed from within. Bodies were on display.

Back To Nature

The fashion world's growing interest in nudity continued into the 1970s except this time it was not so much a symbol of revolution as one of liberation. Although the 1970s are often associated with the emergence of the feminist movement, the fashion world's nod towards the equality-seeking woman manifested itself by harking back to nature. The sharp A-line silhouette and the mini-skirt were replaced by long, floor-skimming skirts and floating dresses and the monotone prints in space-age colours were muted into pastels before exploding into psychedelic prints and flower-power patterns.

The look was one of a 'natural' beauty, an organic, free-flowing style unencumbered by heavy underwear. Underwear manufacturers began making bras with the aim of making them invisible when worn under clothes. The heavy stitching and lifting was replaced with a simpler design made in lighter fabrics, so much so that often the nipple could be clearly defined. This in itself was another development in shape as up until the 1970s, the nipple rarely made an appearance unless accompanied by the unveiling of the entire breast. Nipples were previously suppressed by fabric so no matter how harsh the weather, they very rarely stood out in a crowd.

The 1970s embraced the natural body and it became fashionable to abandon the bra completely. Although this notion of being braless has been hi-jacked and super-imposed upon a feminist movement that supposedly encouraged women not just to remove their underwear but to burn it as a symbol of their liberation, it was in fact more popularly demonstrated as a fashion statement. It wasn't just movie stars and fashion models who abandoned their bras, it was not uncommon for everyday women to walk braless.

Regardless of political however, it is certain that woman look better in young and the flat- fashion flow, the high up to the challenge and more lightweight than became a thing of the past supported by fabric alone.

> **The notion of being braless has been hijacked and superimposed on the feminist movement**

beliefs and notions of comfort the right bra makes a her clothes. So while the chested went with the street once again stepped introduced a range of bras ever before. Underwiring and women's breasts were

It was around this time that American lingerie manufacturer Playtex came to the fore, owned by the Sara Lee Corporation and named after the daughter of the founder, Charles Lubin. Originally specialising in baked goods, the company diversified into underwear and now has a number of lingerie labels including Bali, Glamorise and Just My Size. One of the famous Playtex designs was Cross Your Heart, a non-wired bra that provided ample support due to its broad shoulder straps and cup design.

But the catwalks and magazines were promoting a shape and look that most women could not follow. The nubile, free-flowing silhouette was dependent upon the gene pool and no amount of 'Cross Your Heart' stitching was going to make a difference. The majority had to be selective about how they chose to interpret fashion because their natural shape literally could not keep up.

Muscle-Bound

The vogue for nudity which began in earnest during the 1970s has continued unabated to the present day; for example, very few individuals who have been deemed 'celebrities' have been admitted into this club without baring their bodies.

No sooner had the 1970s acknowledged the beauty of the so-called natural body, than the 1980s rediscovered the benefits of controlling the wayward female form. This time it was not through whalebone, stays or even underwired bras, the fashion world had discovered a whole new mode of corsetry: muscle.

Physical fitness and bodybuilding became a mainstream trend, perhaps due to: the influence of the dance culture popularised by movies such as *Fame* and *Flashdance*; a greater awareness of the health benefits of exercise; and the increased desire to put the body on show. Whatever the reason, men and women began to sculpt their bodies.

An angular, toughened and toned body was the reward promised to those who endured the gruelling exercise routines barked out by a miked-up instructor against a background of pumping dance music. The *Jane Fonda Work Out* books and accompanying tapes began to fly off the shelves as women became intent on toning their thighs and flattening their stomachs. Lycra leotards, leggings and trainers were the uniform for this boot camp atmosphere of star jumps and splits on demand. Body shape control had become internalised – your perfect 'natural' shape was yours to be won by determination and endurance. No pain no gain.

Sports bras became an essential form of support for women striving towards their perfect figure. The heavily-elasticised garments guaranteed ultimate control; nothing less would satisfy a woman determined to improve her physique.

While the 'ideal' shape of the 1960s and the 1970s was far removed from the reality of most women's bodies, the 1980s trend in exercise brought most women some way towards resembling the fashionable physique. This ability to achieve was also reflected in their growing influence within the workplace and society as a whole. Whether it was a career, a home, a family or a look – now more so than ever before, they had the means to get it.

Lingerie designers chose to reflect this emerging 'Superwoman' by focusing on her sexual allure. While clothing designers were arming women with shoulder-padded blouses and jackets, underwear became soft and unstructured. Almost as an antidote to the masculine edge of the fashionable working wardrobe, the woman underneath accentuated her sexuality. Underwear was worn in strong colours like black, red and purple. Not only was this style of lingerie alluring, but with its transparent lace, high-leg pants and teddies it was almost predatory. This was underwear designed to reveal the strong body beneath.

Madonna is responsible for many shifts in underwear fashion. When she first emerged on to the pop scene shamelessly baring her midriff and with bra-straps which were carefully positioned to peek out from underneath the shoulders of tank tops, she started the trend for wearing underwear as outerwear. In her movie, *Desperately Seeking Susan*, she brazenly parades in a pair of men's boxer shorts teamed with white lace stockings and suspenders. Similarly, as her career progressed, she abandoned her softer figure for a gym-honed muscular physique first unveiled during her Who's That Girl tour in 1987. Madonna's arduous fitness regime became part of her cachet and she famously courted the attention of the public and media while jogging with her entourage through the parks of various capital cities, exhausting the panting journalists who trailed in her wake.

While exercise and personal fitness were options for most women, the 'body' that was pitched as the desired shape towards the end of the 1980s was beyond even the most determined of gym fanatics. The rise of the 'supermodel' further enshrined the difference between 'them' and 'us'. This new elite, including Naomi Campbell, Linda Evangelista, Cindy Crawford and Christy Turlington, was established as not only a cut above the average model but in a league all of their own. Their faces and bodies became omnipresent as they fronted international advertising campaigns and music videos; their very presence became an endorsement of success and desirability. Their beauty brought them wealth, fame and status as never before; at one point Linda Evangelista famously remarked that she did not get out of bed for less that $10,000 per day.

As though in keeping with their elite status, their 'supermodel' shape and figure was never something the average woman could expect to achieve; Elle Macpherson was even nicknamed 'The Body' so outstanding was her physique perceived to be. While the 'supermodel' occupied an almost divine status among popular culture for a brief period, she was never presented as an example of how women should actually be. They were crowned with such physical perfection as no ordinary woman could ever hope to attain.

Waifs and Wonderbras

As if in rebellion against the muscle-bound strength of the 1980s, the following decade brought with it the re-emergence of the waif, most notably in the form of model Kate Moss. The teenage model possessed an ethereal fragility not seen since Twiggy and, like her 1960s predecessor, Moss was precariously thin with bird-like legs that looked as though they might snap beneath her. Despite her fragile physique however, Moss embodied a strong, new look that was in stark contrast to the affluence and strength that had dominated fashion for so long. The fashion shoot photographed by Corinne Day which appeared in the directional magazine *ID* simultaneously launched Moss' career and established a trend that was to persevere for most of the following decade.

Grunge had taken hold of fashion and the 'heroin-chic' style portraits of limp-limbed models with hollow eyes and dilated pupils staring vacantly into the camera effectively subverted the smooth image of supermodel perfection. This reversal to a gritty, unpolished image was further proof of fashion's rediscovered interest in youth. The grown-up glamour of the 1980s was replaced with a shabby aesthetic designed to adorn a childlike physique.

The grunge look resurrected the fashion for frail figures not seen since the 1960s.

The female shape has always been a topic for public debate but never before had the shape of a woman's body been such an important indicator of her fashionable, social and political status. Actresses, models, politicians and the new breed of celebrity all began to shrink visibly. A cursory comparison between today's fashion magazines and those of fifteen years ago is startling: the ideal shape now worthy of display has become unmistakably thinner.

The only area which has been permitted to grow is the chest: while legs, arms and hips have diminished to boy-child proportions, breasts have re- mained voluptuous and, if anything, have increased in size courtesy of the growing availability of cosmetic surgery.

Fashion's preference for thin bodies has been portrayed as the most desirable shape even though it is both un- natural and beyond the reach of most women whose natural physical shape cannot comply with this for- mula of stick-thin limbs and swollen breasts. This might go some way towards explaining the popularity of the Wonderbra, renowned for its uplifting capabilities, as even the droopiest and flattest of chests can be transformed into an impressive cleavage courtesy of its padded engineering.

> **Grunge and 'heroin-chic' subverted the smooth image of supermodel perfection**

During the last ten years, the physique promoted as the ideal figure has never been further from the reality of most women's bodies. While census reports repeatedly tell us that we have become taller, heavier and more likely to be obese, the 'ideal' is smaller, thinner, more fragile, and therefore placed even further from our grasp.

In years gone by, the fashionable form was dependent on corsetry, but more recent trends have stipulated that we remove our structured clothing and work from within, regardless of how impossible this may be to achieve. The overall look has been decreed as sexually attractive and therefore feminine, as regards the heterosexual gaze. However, this image could not be further removed from the natural woman and her fertile body. Stick-thin torsos with swollen, nipple-less breasts are not the figures mothers are made of and what is considered sexually attractive ignores many aspects of the body that are natural and make it essentially feminine. Lingerie labels such as La Perla and Gossard have even gone to the lengths of producing a thong specially designed to showcase the Brazilian bikini wax. In the fifteenth century men often wore clothing designed to draw attention to their genitalia as a sign of their virility. Six hundred years later women are doing the same, although the exposure is not an indication of fertility but rather sexuality without the strings attached.

As a result there has been a growing sense of distance between what is considered to be leading fashion and the high street. The most successful retailers are those that specialise in cheap clothing that is influenced more by the ever-changing line-up of 'celebrities' than by the catwalks of Milan and Paris.

While young girls almost certainly want to dress like their idols, they fulfil this desire by carrying designer handbags and wearing similar shoes, make-up and hair. Clothing has become dispensable, bought for next to nothing and worn for no longer than a few months.

Current fashion has left its mark most perceptibly upon our body-obsessed culture. Magazine and newspapers devote huge amounts of coverage to the figures of celebrities and the various fad diets that have helped them achieve their supposed physical perfection. It would seem weight is indirectly proportional to fame; actresses like Jennifer Aniston and Nicole Kidman have become thinner as their stars have shone brighter.

Fashionable underwear is no longer charged with providing shape but instead acts as a showcase for the physical 'ideal', whether the everyday woman possesses such a figure or not. For over a century women have been warned against their underwear; it has been portrayed as a health risk, a symbol of social repression and has even been identified as a source of physical discomfort. But yet women everywhere continue to wear it in all its forms, fashionable or otherwise.

> *There can be no fashion without foundation.*

Chapter Two
Fashion

L ingerie, regardless of how brief or insubstantial, is one of the most important elements of an outfit. From Christian Dior's New Look to Donatella Versace's stomach-grazing necklines, fashion has relied upon the right kind of underwear. It might be a Chanel boucle suit hanging in the wardrobe but it won't achieve its intended shape and silhouette on the body all by itself. A beautiful dress worn without the appropriate underwear is like a building without any foundations – sooner or later it's going to buckle or lean ever so slightly to one side.

Yves Saint Laurent once remarked that there could be no fashion without foundation and although he wasn't referring to underwear at the time, a woman would be hard pressed to slip into one of his body-skimming 1970s safari-inspired trouser suits without a pair of sheer knickers.

It is only in recent decades that lingerie designers have earned notoriety, partially due to celebrity endorsement from models-turned-lingerie-designers like Caprice and Elle Macpherson and popstars like Kylie Minogue and Jennifer Lopez. Previously underwear producers were seen as manufacturers, responsible for the production of a much-needed, functional garment. Their role was not considered to be an artistic one although without their skills many of the garments created by high fashion could not be worn by anyone other than catwalk models. The emergence of the fashionable boyish physique during the 1920s did not miraculously coincide with a generation of flat-chested women; the lean silhouette associated with the flapper style was largely owing to the minimising effect of bust bodice. Similarly, the hourglass figure made desirable by Christian Dior's New Look in 1947 simply could not have been achieved without the aid of a waspie girdle.

This new-found respect for lingerie designers is perhaps also due to the modern desire to wear our underwear on the outside and the growing acceptance of partial or complete nudity in magazines, newspapers and advertising.

Fashion reflects the culture in which it is created and by extension underwear is also a kind of social barometer. The range of styles available today is so diverse that decisions made in the lingerie department reflect the personality and lifestyle of the buyer. When faced with sport-bras, push-up bras, minimising bras, seamless bras, panties with ribbons, panties with bottom-cleavage padding, crotchless thongs, white cotton bikini briefs – all of which are available along a city high street – the final purchase provides an insight into the woman herself.

Whalebone Women

At the turn of the twentieth century a woman's underclothes played a crucial role in her wardrobe because without the stays and whalebone of the corset she simply could not manipulate her body into the shape for which fashionable clothes were made.

While fashion and the rails of the high street now cater for a variety of shapes and sizes, designers at the beginning of the twentieth century did not make such concessions. Certainly not all women were of the same dimensions, but with the aid of a corset they could achieve a size and shape far removed from that which Mother Nature had intended.

At the beginning of the twentieth century the Edwardian era had brought about a previously unseen degree of eroticism. Manufacturers began to adorn underwear with decorative lace and ribbon as they came to be seen as sexually alluring items of clothing. Underwear was given the new title of 'lingerie' and frivolous terms such as 'knickers' were gradually incorporated into the wardrobe lexicon. Fashion magazines began devoting editorial content to the positive influence a good corset could exert upon a woman's posture and alignment.

The corset was of course only one item among a range of underclothes worn by women of this period. Personal hygiene had become a concern and it was believed that outer clothing (i.e. dresses, skirts and shirtwaists) required protection from the body and all its supposedly filthy secretions. Traditionally, a chemise, or 'combinations' of chemise and drawers (which originated in the 1860s) were worn underneath the corset as a barrier between it and the skin. The chemise usually had a front or a back fastening and came up as high as the neck or, in the case of evening-wear, was often sleeveless with a plunging neckline.

The Parisian couturier, Paul Poiret, had become a leading light in the fashion industry by the early years of the twentieth century. Not only is he considered to be one of the most influential designers of this era but he was also one of the first couturiers to deliberately mesh his fashions with the work of contemporary artists. Many of his collections were beautifully illustrated by artists like George Lepape and Paul Iribe. Poiret and the artists with whom he collaborated are considered to be among the luminaries of the Art Deco movement. His work drew inspiration from unexpected sources such as eastern European peasant dress and the Ballet Russes. This breadth of vision created a look that encapsulated the changing social attitudes to sexuality and desire.

Poiret was an accomplished self-publicist and his determination to liberate women from their corsetry became both his obsession (his *ideé fixe*) and a lucrative advertising ploy. Even as a trainee designer working in La Maison Worth, the established fashion house of Charles Worth, Poiret had been obsessed with removing the curves from women's dress and replacing them with a more simplistic, straight silhouette. In 1912, inspired by the work of Cubist artists such as Pablo Picasso and Georges Braque, he translated their linear forms into his collection which was characterised by long, column-shaped dresses and soft, empire waistlines. His designs were met with critical acclaim and without further ado, Poiret declared: 'The corset is dead.'

> **The austerity of war made layers of petticoats and flounce appear frivolous**

Writing in his autobiography many years later, Poiret reflected on how he had liberated women from their restrictive corsets and congratulated himself on providing women with a dramatic new shape:

The last representative of this abominable apparatus was called the Gache Sarraute. It divided the wearer into two distinct masses: on the one side there was the bust and bosom, on the other, the whole behindward aspect, so that the lady looked as if she were hauling a trailer. It was almost a return to the bustle. Like all the great revolutions, that one had been made in the name of Liberty – to give free play to the abdomen: it was equally in the name of Liberty that I proclaimed the fall of the corset and the adoption of the brassiere which, since then, has won the day.

In the years preceding the First World War clothing in general became simplified: the straighter lines favoured by Poiret and his counterparts had reduced the need for the exaggerated hourglass shape popularised by the Edwardian era and, as a result, layers of underclothes became redundant.

As the men were shipped off to war women were called upon to make their contribution to the war effort. Fashion could not help but be affected by the mood of sorrow and tragedy and the flounce and frills that had dominated the skirts of women a decade before were abandoned for a straighter, more sombre style.

Although the corset was still an integral garment, cami-knickers – a shorter version of combinations (a garment which covered the whole body, including legs and arms) – were worn to protect a lady's modesty in place of petticoats. The austerity of war had made layers of petticoats and flounce appear frivolous. Practicality was the order of the day and who had the time or the inclination or indeed the servants to launder and starch layers and layers of petticoat?

Boom but no Bust

The post-war years marked a fresh new era of peace and the economic boom that followed fuelled a desire for new ideas and a general shake-up of social mores and attitudes. Traditional social constructs came under fresh scrutiny from a young generation armed with a new understanding of sex and morality influenced by affluence, the advancement of technology, and cinema. A new demographic was gaining a foothold in society: between childhood and marriage stretched youth.

This generation needed a new style, a radically different mode of dress that would break the mould cast by their war-ravaged parents. The fashion industry came up with a whole new fabric of costume – the skin. The Roaring Twenties, as they were subsequently nicknamed, witnessed the most fundamental changes in women's dress the modern world had ever seen. Hemlines were raised to just below the knee and the neckline of evening gowns plunged at the front and the back – never before had such an expanse of flesh been on display.

Women had already begun to wear their hair short. Paul Poiret had cut his models' hair in 1908, the writer Colette had also sacrificed her long braids in favour of a bob and, in 1917, Gabrielle 'Coco' Chanel announced it was time to cut her long tresses. She cropped not only her own hair but also that of her in-house models although various biographers have speculated that a domestic accident involving a water-heater before an evening at the opera was the real reason for the mass shearing.

A wave of new cosmetics and skin products began to flood the market. Women were bathing and oiling their bodies with a range of lotions and 'vanishing creams';

they even began applying false tan. For centuries bronzed skin had been associated with hard labour and poverty while lily-white complexions were a symbol of wealth and privilege. Coco Chanel is believed to have started this tanned trend when she returned to her Parisian atelier after a summer on the French coast sporting a sun-kissed glow. No sooner had well-known sophisticates like Chanel begun parading their bronzed bodies, than the suntan became synonymous with style, affluence and travel.

Designers such as Jeanne Lanvin, Chanel and Elsa Schiaperelli began working with plain fabrics as canvases for intricate embroidered adornments and beading. This was partly due to the influence of folk art and the ongoing fascination with the Orient but was also the result of a shortage of textiles following the First World War. Variety of material was limited which led designers to compensate with elaborate em-broidered panels, sequins and accessories.

Coco Chanel included a number of Slavic-inspired embellishments in her collec-tions – particularly during her romantic affair with the Grand Duke Dmitri Pavlo-vitch, grandson of Czar Alexander II. He, along with most of the Russian nobility who survived the Bolshevik revolution, had been exiled after the 1917 revolution. They arrived in Paris completely impoverished only to be rescued by Chanel and other quick-witted fashion designers who capitalised on the skilful fingers of the noblewomen. Ironically, it was motifs taken from the style of the revolutionaries that Chanel and many of her contemporaries required the penniless Russian nobility to recreate.

In keeping with this entirely new female wardrobe, underwear was also subject to an overhaul. The new love affair with exposed flesh resulted in a reduction in the number and bulk of underclothes. Furthermore, shorter skirts and dropped waists had created an altogether more boyish physique that was utterly removed from the curvaceous figures and waist-tightening corsets of previous decades.

The androgynous shape and 'flapper-style' dresses still required a figure that did not come naturally. This presented most women with a dilemma which was brilliantly illustrated by Julie Andrews in the movie, *Thoroughly Modern Millie*. At one point in the film the heroine attempts to emulate the look by bobbing her hair and taking up her skirts. It is only when she attempts to hang a long string of beads down her chest that she realises her voluptuous bosom is not part of the new vogue. Brassieres and girdles, not to mention bust bodices, became very tight during this period and were employed to produce the desired flat chest.

The 1920s corset, at this stage made with woven elastic, was wrapped around the hips to extend the narrow silhouette. Women also took to wearing all-in-one 'cami-knickers' or 'chemise-knickers' which were worn beneath the corset. The knickers remained open like a skirt, and hung down in points as low as the knee. As a substitute for the corset, some women opted to wear the 'belt', which came with or without boning. Those without boning were made of elastic only and were known as 'roll-ons' simply because that was how they were put on; those with zippers were called 'step-ins'.

Towards the end of the decade, knickers or drawers were shortened significantly to accommodate the shorter hemlines and were referred to as 'panties' or 'briefs'. The most common material used was artificial silk, primarily because it was widely available, although for the more expensive tastes, fabrics such as satin, crepe de chine and occasionally voile were also popular.

Not only was underwear responsible for creating a different body shape, it also had to become less obtrusive; discretion became highly desirable and manufacturers began to minimise the number of seams and fastenings. Such changes were remarked upon in a 1924 edition of *Vogue*:

> *The creaseless perfection can only be acquired by wearing a minimum of clothing beneath. What would our grandmothers have thought of limiting them, with evening dress, to a pair of panties?*

During the second half of the 1920s, the 'Garçonne' look was developed by designers across Europe, particularly by Coco Chanel, Elsa Schiaperelli and Jean Patou. The name was taken from the scandalous novel by Victor Magueritte, *La Garçonne*, a tale of an independent young woman who left her family and village in the hope of finding a better life.

The 'Garçonne' was essentially an androgynous look and was in complete contrast to the sexually-charged femininity which had dominated the Edwardian period only two decades earlier. Womenswear became so simplified that it was churlishly nick-named by designer Paul Poiret as 'pauvreté de luxe' (poverty of luxury). In a celebrated exchange between the two designers, Poiret demanded: 'Who are you mourning for, Mademoiselle Chanel?' To which she replied, 'For you, Monsieur.' Poiret had fallen out of favour following the war and was eclipsed by Coco Chanel who had become known for her simplified suits and narrow colour palette. She preferred to work in jersey, one of the very few materials in plentiful supply after the war. Chanel, always a keen businesswoman, was able to buy it in vast quantities because it had previously only been used in men's sports attire. Some fashion journalists even went so far as to call it a 'soup-kitchen' style. Chanel was undeterred and continued to use the fabric throughout her career; she had every confidence in the elegant sophistication of her clothes.

Hollywood Style

By the 1930s Hollywood had become a major influence upon fashion and style, as stars like Bette Davis, Jean Harlow and Ginger Rogers were idolised by both men and women enraptured by their beauty and glamour. The silver screen beamed a glow of geniality and a dash of romance into the humdrum lives of poor Americans, deflated by the Wall Street Crash of 1929 which destroyed much of the boom and prosperity gained in the 1920s.

Designers began creating clothes structured along the lines of the female shape and evening-wear in particular was often cut along the bias to ensure the fabric hung close to the body. This return to femininity in fashions resulted in a more erotic style of dress; fabrics clung to the figure making it essential that underclothes were as unobtrusive as possible.

Similarly, men's fashions were often dictated by Hollywood, as was shown in the sudden slump in the sale of men's vests following the premiere of Frank Capra's 1934 movie *It Happened One Night* starring Clark Gable and Claudette Colbert. In one scene Gable removed his jacket and shirt to reveal a bare torso and almost overnight department stores across America reported a fall in the sale of men's vests.

Towards the end of the 1930s as Europe once again prepared for war, clothing became decidedly more sombre. The flapper had begun to appear frivolous and the waist-less, childlike dress of the 1920s was replaced with a more grown-up, sedate style.

Women wore broad-shouldered jackets, often exaggerated by the use of padding, and straight skirts that sometimes stretched down to just above the ankle. The look was one of confidence and strength for women who could work, travel and stand on their own two feet.

While day-wear remained uncomplicated and simple, reflecting the thrifty mood of the early 1930s, evening-wear was, by contrast, aspirational. Dresses consisted of strapless bodices and tiny waists above wide skirts of crinoline. Bustled skirts also enjoyed a brief revival during this period in a nod to bygone eras except this time the shape was created with padding instead of hooped skirts and horse-hair petticoats.

During the war years, fashion lay dormant as men and women dressed in uniform and quality clothing was hard to find. Shortages were rife, fashion was cast aside and three weeks after France and Britain declared war on Germany Coco Chanel closed her Parisian atelier and declared that it was not a time for fashion. Most of the individuals working in the industry had fled in fear of the approaching Nazi soldiers as so many of them fell into the social groups Hitler was determined to eradicate.

Waspie Women

The French press were on strike on the day in 1947 when Christian Dior launched his Carolle line and it was in fact the American editor of *Harper's Bazaar*, Carmel Snow, who bestowed on the collection its infamous title of 'The New Look'. This event marked a seismic change in women's fashions, as for decades clothing had steadily become leaner and more stream-lined, with shorter, narrower skirts. The New Look swept all of this minimalism aside and brought back wide, ex-pansive skirts made from yards and yards of luxurious material. The focus was once again directed towards the waist which was cinched in as narrow as it would go.

> **The New Look was one of confidence and strength for women who would work, travel and stand on their own two feet**

Dior said he wanted to make skirts open like the blooming petals of a flower; his designs were imbued with a fragile femininity that had not been seen for almost half a century. The New Look revelled in its excess of fabric and glamour – an antidote to the sobriety of the war-time wardrobe – and almost overnight women's fashion became ultra-feminine and decadently luxurious.

The basic principles of the Carolle line were gradually filtered through to high street dressmakers and boutiques which in turn led to radical changes in the under-wear drawers of women all over the world. Once again underwear was required to create the shape to accommodate fashion. The curve-enhancing corsets which had been cast off by the flappers and hard-working women of the 1930s were reinvented as 'waspie' belt-like corsets and girdles and wrapped around the waists of fashionable ladies everywhere.

Paris was established as the fashion capital of the late 1940s and early 1950s and Hollywood did not hesitate in showcasing this glamorous new style. Studio bosses began commissioning designers to create costumes for entire movies. A famous relationship was that of Hubert de Givenchy and Audrey Hepburn, one of the most trend-setting actresses of the twentieth century.

In one of her early movies, *Sabrina Fair,* Hepburn played the role of a chauffeur's daughter who is sent to Paris to attend cookery school and after two years returns home transformed into a beautiful and elegant young lady dressed from head to toe in Parisian couture. In order to make this transformation credible, Hepburn suggested to her studio bosses that they commission Givenchy to design her entire wardrobe and throughout the film her elegant frame is adorned with the most exquisite dresses. At one point she assures her beloved, played by William Holden, that she has the perfect outfit for that evening's party: 'I have the most beautiful dress with yards and yards of skirt!' she cries with glee before skipping off to begin her preparations.

The fashions of the 1950s also resulted in women giving a great deal of consideration to their busts, the top half of the desirable hourglass figure. While skirts were voluminous, blouses and sweaters were worn as close-fitting as possible and women looked to brassieres to provide them with the best possible shape.

'Fillers' or padding were often employed by women who felt they might be slightly lacking in that area. Some women even resorted to inflatable bras to fill out their physique. In 1953 Triumph introduced a cone-shaped, circular-stitched bra which succeeded in enhancing even the most petite of bosoms. For a brief period, women were encouraged to fill out their figures by following weight-gaining diets and chest-improving exercises. Dior, and the designers who followed his lead, dressed women as though they were exotic, dainty birds, feathered with expansive skirts and teetering on spindly high heels.

One of the few designers not to engage fully with this return to shape-altering fashions was Chanel who had made her name based on the simplicity and functional quality of her designs. Chanel had closed her atelier soon after the Nazi occupation of Paris and spent the war years living in her apartment in the Ritz Hotel. Shortly after the liberation of the French capital, Chanel moved to Switzerland and did not return to Paris until 1954, by which time she was just one of a handful of female designers working in what had become a male-dominated industry. During this period she is reported to have remarked to a fashion journalist: 'Dressing women is not a man's job. They dress them badly because they scorn them.' In an interview with American *Vogue* in 1954 she added, 'Elegance in clothes means freedom to move freely.'

Mini Mania

By 1960 hemlines had risen to an all-time high above the knee and by 1963 they were brushing the mid-thigh. The feminine hourglass form was replaced with a boyish waif-like shape reminiscent of the androgynous look popularised in the 1920s.

Lesley Hornby – better known as Twiggy – became the face of the decade. Her huge eyes and stick-thin physique which prompted the nickname, appeared on billboards and in magazines all over the world. She was considered the ultimate clotheshorse; she modelled for the most famous photographers and was dressed by the most accomplished designers. Her tomboy crop was created by Vidal Sassoon of London and soon women everywhere were shearing their locks. Twiggy's nymphette face and incredibly thin arms and legs epitomised the 1960s look of doe-eyed, boyish simplicity.

Designers such as Mary Quant and Emilio Pucci created waistless A-line dresses that hung from perilously thin shoulders. Drainpipe trousers and baby-doll smock tops were wrapped around childlike bodies. Make-up focused on widening eyes with thick eyeliner and heavy lashes while lips were faded in pale beige and pinks.

> **Twiggy's nymphette face epitomised the 1960s doe-eyed simplicity**

The cinched-in waists of the previous decade were replaced by a rectangular silhouette, and the fashionably thin torsos were left unattended by underwear. The waspies and girdles preferred by women just a few years before were happily dismissed by the younger generation. Mary Quant was one designer who capitalised on this new trend and designed a range of boyish pants and matching vests to accompany her skimpy mini-skirts and dresses.

Naturally most women were not shaped like Twiggy and were unwilling to abandon their figure-shaping undergarments altogether, regardless of fashion or trend. The ongoing sales in structured brassieres and knickers by labels such as Triumph and Berlei – who continued to design and produce whirlpool-stitched bras and long knickers – are testimony to this.

Italian lingerie label La Perla incorporated the ethereal silhouette into their designs but were careful not to forget the reality of the female figure. The photographs from a 1960s catalogue show lithe-limbed women wearing the fashionable neat bras and panties but they have also included a range of high-waisted, long knickers, reminiscent of the cycling shorts worn today. Regardless of fashion, some women still preferred their smalls to be quite substantial.

Natural Beauty

Still intoxicated by the youthful exuberance of the previous decade, the 1970s encouraged women to abandon all the trappings of the previous generations and shed their bras altogether. On her wedding day Bianca Jagger was photographed seated in the town hall of St Tropez wearing a white trouser suit, the jacket nipped in at the waist, but clearly revealing that she was wearing very little underneath.

The then unknown beauty, who subsequently made a name for herself as a human rights activist and environmental campaigner, was suddenly thrust into the limelight following her marriage to Rolling Stones lead singer, Mick Jagger. Years later, during an interview with *Vogue* magazine in 1974, she remarked she was 'the only person to have become a star without doing anything at all'.

During this period the women's movement was gathering momentum; rallies and marches were held all over the world calling for equal pay and abortion legislation. The fashion world responded by injecting a distinctly masculine flavour into women's clothing. Yves Saint Laurent, who had already created 'Le Smoking' – his womenswear equivalent of the tuxedo – continued in this vein and much of his collections were dominated by soft masculine tailoring such as the safari-style jacket and skirt.

The feminist calls for equality were also reflected in the clothing of American designer Ralph Lauren, who began dressing women in slacks and waistcoats. Lauren first became known for his menswear and it was only in the 1970s that he began translating his trademark 'all-American boy' style into women's clothing. He also designed a large proportion of the wardrobe for the movie of F. Scott Fitzgerald's 1920s novel, *The Great Gatsby,* and he dressed Diane Keaton for her starring role in Woody Allen's 1977 hit movie, *Annie Hall.* No sooner had the lines formed outside the movie theatres than women everywhere began wearing men's chinos and over-sized shirts with neck-ties that were carefully askew. As feminist activists pounded the pavements, fashion had synchronised with their desire for equality.

Coinciding with this distancing from the strictly feminine lines of previous decades, lingerie began to reflect the growing reluctance among young women to contort their bodies into shapes far removed from their natural form.

French designer Emmanuelle Khanh famously announced in the late 1960s: 'Couture is dead.' Her rebellious nature was reflected in her clothing, heavily dominated by street fashion and reminiscent of the brands created by Mary Quant and Biba in London a few years before. Previously a model for Balanciaga, she rejected the trussed-up, hourglass shape that had dominated so much of the 1950s and early 1960s fashion, preferring instead to recreate the free-moving style of the 1920s and 1930s.

Khanh also produced a line of lingerie, characterised by brightly coloured bras and pants, totally without structure or underwiring and decorated with floral motifs.

Her designs encapsulated the fresh-faced innocence the fashion world was keen to create. The free-thinking, free-love-making younger generation did not feel the need for girdles and bust-improving brassieres.

It was during the 1970s that Italian lingerie label La Perla began researching and analysing trends in female attitudes towards underwear and clothing. They translated their research into designs that were in keeping with the liberated times but simultaneously provided the physical support required. The Italian manufacturer oversaw lengthy testing and development of new elastomere fibres such as lycra and wove it into their silks, tulles and lace thus ensuring the body was softly supported without the use of heavy underwire or thick elastic.

It was also during this decade that the Australian underwear label Sloggi became an internationally-recognised brand. Sloggi first entered the market when Triumph International patented a fabric called corespun – a mix of cotton and lycra, which they incorporated into their cotton briefs. Sloggi's broad range of styles (Sloggi was also the creator of the 'Tai'– a combination of the g-string and the tanga brief), combined with their trademark waistband, has proved extremely popular and the label continues to fill the underwear drawers of men and women all over the world.

Sexed Up and On Display

The catwalk displays during the 1980s had one common theme: work. Women were making their mark and were joining and returning to the workforce in droves.

Previously fashion designers had con-centrated on day and night, sports activities and even travel but never before had such focus been directed at the wardrobe of the working woman.

'Power-dressing' as it became known, provided a wardrobe of armour for the female executive, the professional who was considered both womanly and, very obviously, the boss. Fashion designers created a new silhouette to suit this seemingly contradictory image for women, and the 'power suit' became the staple uniform of the working woman.

> **Power-dressing provided a wardrobe of armour for the female executive**

Jackets were broad-shoul-dered and reinforced with padding to create a sharp, strong line indicating that the woman underneath meant business. This masculine top half was balanced by a close-fitting double-breasted fastening at the waist and a short, narrow skirt. The idealised shape was essentially triangular; long slim legs protruding from the square-set shoulder-padded armour as though to placate the male of the species should he feel unnerved – these fragile, feminine legs could still buckle if required.

The 1980s has been derided by many fashion editors as an era without grace or style but it is important to bear in mind that designers working in this period were traversing new territory. Women were expected to achieve both at work and at home and they demanded more from their clothing because the world was expecting more from them. By peering into the lingerie drawers of the fashionable women of the 1980s, the contrasting roles of successful professional and traditional wife/mother/girlfriend is clearly manifested in the style of their underwear.

The soft, deconstructed cottons of the late 1960s and 1970s were replaced with black satin and lace, and the skimpy, uncomplicated panties were abandoned in favour of intricate combinations of suspender belts and stockings. These garments served many diverse purposes ranging from support and function to allure and seduction.

Photographer Helmut Newton often pictured women dressed in their underwear. His images feature tall, lithe, almost Amazonian women, dressed in full-length coats unbuttoned to reveal their black lingerie. They were often captured striding confidently towards the camera. Newton's images of strength and sexuality seemed to extol the essence of the 1980s woman.

La Perla introduced their first 'body-suit' in 1983, a stretch garment made entirely of lace and the forerunner to the numerous variations of the style known as the 'body' that were later worn as outerwear, under jackets and invariably with trousers or jeans.

By the end of the decade, underwear had become outerwear, fashion was peeling off the layers and lingerie acted as a display case for the body beneath. While this was a significant development in the relationship between women and their underwear it was not the first time a woman's underclothes had been worn particularly for display purposes. For much of the eighteenth century colourful silk and satin petticoats were seen peeking out from underneath hooped skirts. In the 1920s, although it was not part of the overall look, it was considered quite acceptable to accidentally reveal when seated a few inches of knee-length knickers from underneath the shorter hemline.

These fashionable and perhaps even rather endearing indiscretions were very modest in comparison to the provocative look championed by stars like Madonna in the mid 1980s. Famed for her unique style and ability to identify new looks and trends, Madonna's vampish image first entered the mainstream when her second single 'Holiday' went to the top of the American Billboard Charts in 1983.

Her individual style of displayed black lace brassiere straps, bangles and crucifixes sparked a trend and young girls and women immediately began wearing clothes made from fabrics traditionally associated with underwear. Madonna took this one step further on the cover of her second album, *Like a Virgin*, where she posed reclining on a bridal bed, as though eagerly anticipating the arrival of a lover, fully dressed in her wedding lingerie.

While mainstream fashion carried this trend it was mostly worn by the very young. It was also still evident in the wardrobe of the working woman who would often wear a lace-trimmed 'body' underneath a business suit. High street stores, such as Dorothy Perkins and Principles, did a steady line in beaded and embroidered camisoles which provided the all-important feminine touch.

Although lingerie had become more intricate and fanciful, it did not exert the same control over the body that previous styles of underwear had achieved. Instead, the shape of the body was to be achieved by physical exercise and diet. The increasing desire to flaunt bare flesh resulted in a more body-conscious society who honed their physique in gyms and aerobics classes.

Underwear as Outerwear

Four years after her *Like a Virgin* album Madonna once again launched a new trend when she wore Jean-Paul Gaultier's soft pink satin bustier during her Blonde Ambition tour in 1989.

While Gaultier may have earned greater mainstream acclaim due to his association with Madonna, many designers were also using exaggerated forms of traditional female underwear as part of their collections. Thierry Mugler created a bustier in the style of a car bonnet complete with silver wing-mirrors which protruded from either side and was immortalised in pop-singer George Michael's music video for the song, 'Too Funky'.

Mainstream media welcomed this witty interpretation of old-fashioned underwear although a number of esteemed fashion critics severely criticised the designers for their catwalk portrayal of the female figure. *The Sunday Times* fashion editor, Colin McDowell, considered that:

Many homosexual designers are repulsed by the female breast as the outward and visible sign of the motherhood which destroys the perfection of the female figure even as it menaces their own sexual world; they hide their fear in laughter, by making fun of them and the femininity they signify. Conical bras, outrageously pointed and bearing no relationship to the shape of real breasts, are a cruel joke that brings women into the world of the crudest female impersonators, and puts them on the same level as the rugby player with coconuts under his jersey.

Although Gaultier and Madonna have been heralded as chiefly responsible for the return of the corset, designers such as Vivienne Westwood had been fashioning basques for a number of years. Westwood had evoked the corsetry of the early twentieth century in many of her designs, and fashion writers have repeatedly cited her reinvention of this garment as her most important contribution to fashion. In her 1987 Harris Tweed collection she featured a white and powder blue bustier which she said was inspired by the sensuality of French rococo.

Westwood and Gaultier reintroduced the corset as outerwear as a symbol of female empowerment, subverting the commonly-held belief that it was an example of repression. The impact upon lingerie was dramatic: the heavily struc- tured underwired brassiere became the dominant style practically overnight.

> "Westwood reintroduced the corset as a symbol of female empower-ment"

The re-emergence of cor- setry and its subsequent influence upon lingerie fashion stimulated much debate; numerous inches of newsprint were devoted to the pros and cons, meanwhile depart- ment stores across the world were bulging with underwired bras.

Not only had high fashion made its mark on everyday underwear, the love affair with the corset had left its mark on the body itself. Women everywhere were determined that no matter how meagre or tired their busts might be, the moment they put on their bras their breasts would be held aloft and, most importantly, together.

The Wonderbra was the salvation for many a woman whose bosom did not live up to expectation. In the early 1990s, Gossard's licence to produce the Wonderbra expired and Playtex, an American underwear giant, bought it and relaunched the bra using Czech model Eva Herzigova and the famous 'Hello Boys' campaign.

The promotion was a resounding success, Herzigova's cleavage adorned billboards all over the world and the combination of self-possessed sexuality and the championing of a new fashionable shape struck a chord with women everywhere. In 1994 New York department store Macy's was selling 3,000 Wonderbras a day.

Just as fashion had begun to hark back to the underwear of the past by redefining the corset, the Wonderbra was imposing the shape-altering effects, albeit to a lesser degree, favoured by previous generations.

Each season would see the revival of another decade along the catwalk. No sooner were the short dresses of the 1960s reinvented by Karl Lagerfeld at Chanel but the bell-bottomed flares of the 1970s were sported by pop acts from S Express to the Spice Girls.

House music had taken hold of the younger generation in Britain as nightclubs, beaches and abandoned barns scattered throughout the countryside hosted all-night raves. Leisure wear had made a significant impact upon street fashion, and tracksuits, halter-neck tops and hot pants adorned sweat-drenched bodies as they moved en masse to the hypnotic throb of dance music.

While Madonna's style had filled lingerie departments with more underwiring than they had seen for decades there was also a growing trend for seamless, subtle underwear. As part of the grunge rejection of ostentatious clothing and labels that had dominated the 1980s, one designer had his finger on the pulse.

Shortly after her infamous photo shoot with Corinne Day, the waif-like Kate Moss was snapped up by American designer Calvin Klein. Moss would become one of the most successful models in the world; her fragile frame and make-up free face seemed to embody everything the designer wanted his clothing and fragrances to portray. In her first advertisement for the perfume, Obsession, she appeared barefoot, wide-eyed and seemingly devoid of frippery and affectation. In a further advertisement for CKBe, she reminded the audience to 'Just be'.

Moss also promoted Klein's underwear line, a range of simple cotton bras and panties, ideal for a waifish body like hers but not suited for the more voluptuous figure. However, his simplistic style was disseminated to the high street and lingerie designers began introducing 'nude' ranges. Women's underwear reclaimed a degree of intimacy that was not available to those wearing dramatic shape-enhancers like the Wonderbra.

Strip to be Seen

As the new millennium beckoned, fashion was never so determined to peel away layers of clothing. British designer Matthew Williamson had made his name creating evening dresses so scant that he even went so far as to incorporate matching underwear into his garments. Actress and model Kelly Brook made a name for herself when she attended the London movie premiere of *Snatch* wearing a sparkling pink Williamson dress which left so little to the imagination that she appeared on the front page of every tabloid newspaper the next morning.

Sex and celebrity have become the marketing executive's favourite ploys and numerous lingerie labels have used famous faces (and bodies) to promote their products. Before launching her own range of underwear, pop star Kylie Minogue starred in an advertisement for the up-market lingerie label, Agent Provocateur. The commercial was shown in cinemas only and featured the Antipodean singer wearing stockings and suspenders astride a bucking bronco. The commercial was subsequently deemed so risqué by film censors that it was shown only in theatres screening adult movies.

Celebrities such as Elle Macpherson, Caprice and Jennifer Lopez have all launched their own lines of underwear, none of which is particularly groundbreaking in style or structure and is largely noteworthy because of the famous face which adorns the label.

The twentieth and early twenty-first centuries have seen more radical developments in the style of underwear than any other. In 1900 women were trussed-up in heavy layers of underclothes and by the dawn of the new millennium, they were wearing scant thongs and push-up bras. Today, lingerie is as much a fashion accessory as a handbag or piece of jewellery. Although it is not always on display to the same extent as outer clothing, many women are as keen to have a designer label on their bra as they are to have one on their jeans.

Contemporary dress and, in particular, casual clothing, can often be worn with little or no underwear. Naturally, most women opt for some form of physical support but an underwired bra is by no means an integral element to an outfit consisting of denim jeans and a shirt. This is perhaps well illustrated by a dress from Alexander McQueen's 2005 Spring/Summer collection which features a corset as part of its design. The dress is loose-fitting and, although the corset is incorporated into the exterior of the dress, with suspender straps dangling below the waist, it is by no means restrictive. McQueen has reinvented the corset as a decorative embellishment; its shape-defining properties are completely redundant.

Although the supposedly ideal female shape has always been intrinsically linked to the fashion of the day, the modern woman is not expected to dramatically transform her natural physique using restrictive undergarments. The body sculpting that was once achieved through corsetry is now cultivated by dieting and exercise. Fashionable underwear has given up creating the idealised shape which has gone beyond the bounds of possibility for most women anyway and instead focuses upon a lifestyle that lingerie will supposedly help create. Previously underwear was full of promise of what it could do for the woman underneath. Today lingerie carries a promise of what the woman may do while wearing it.

> *It is no coincidence that the independent, free-thinking modern woman is not encased in whalebone.*

Chapter Three
Politics

How political is your underwear? While perusing lingerie in a department store you are unlikely to consider the valiant women before you who campaigned for the right to vote and work. It is doubtful that your ancestral sisters' journey to emancipation is at the forefront of your mind when considering 'low-rise' bikini briefs and 'uplift' bras and why should it be? What on earth did their hunger-strikes and imprisonment have to do with today's choice between underwired or non-wired bras? Everything.

You may or may not realise this when making a decision between a pair of lace embroidered shorts and a satin thong but without the efforts of our suffragist ancestors, the selection of underwear available today would be dramatically different. It is no coincidence that the independent, free-thinking modern woman is not encased in whalebone and it's not just because La Perla and Marks and Spencer say so either. Women's role in society has changed more significantly during the last one hundred years than it has during any other period in history and as women have changed, so has their underwear.

The fashion of underwear is a reflection of the times we live in and the wide variety of styles available along the high street is evidence of the type of life a woman can choose for herself. Today's woman is working, resting, exercising, mothering, seducing and, if she is particularly fortunate, all in the same day. Even if she doesn't do half of that, she still has a host of activities and expectations to fulfil and one design of lingerie simply isn't going to cut it.

A typical department store has a lingerie section with a variety of styles, from uplift bras and diamanté thongs to traditional girdles and support knickers, as women today come in all shapes and sizes and from all walks of life. Different women have different requirements.

Undoubtedly you will be considering what you intend or hope to do while choosing a particular design of lingerie – work, exercise, socialising – whatever it may be, your choice is dependent upon your activity. Who wants to attend a black-tie ball wearing a bulky sports bra? In the same vein, you are unlikely to waste the benefits of a Vivienne Westwood basque while walking your dog or running on the treadmill.

Ladies, Land and Lingerie

But it wasn't always so. A hundred years ago, a woman's choice of activities was significantly limited and inextricably linked to her social position. As the twentieth century dawned in Ireland, women were entirely dependent upon their fathers and husbands to provide a roof over their heads and sustenance in their bodies.

In 1876, Anna Haslam, originally from Youghal, Co. Cork, and her husband, Thomas, formed the first Irish suffrage society – the Dublin Women's Suffrage Association (later to become the Irish Women's Suffrage Association). The members were drawn mainly from the Society of Friends and their primary objective was to improve land rights for women thus ensuring they were no longer disinherited by their husbands and brothers.

The IWSA were adamantly non-violent and determined to use the Irish constitution and political lobbying to achieve their goal. So resolute were they that a number of years later Frank Sheehy Skeffington, a renowned Irish nationalist and respected public figure, described them as the 'pioneers of feminism in Ireland'.

> " Women were entirely dependent on their fathers and husbands "

Before long the IWSA had gathered steam and as their influence stretched further afield, they became known as the Irish Women's Suffrage and Local Government Association (IWSLGA). Thomas and Anna Haslam continued to campaign for political reform and an end to discrimination against women; in addition to equal property rights they agitated for better education opportunities and an extension of the local government vote for women.

The wardrobe of a woman such as Anna Haslam would have been largely influenced by the fashions in London which were usually relayed to the well-to-do women of Ireland through the pages of monthly periodicals such as *Lady of the House*, a magazine read by women throughout Ireland and England.

The magazine focused on informing wealthy members of Anglo-Irish society of the whereabouts and activities of their class. The January 1909 edition featured a 'National Gallery of Irish Celebrities of the Past'. Out of one hundred people there were seven women, including Maria Edgeworth – author of *Letters for Literary Ladies*, a fictional collection of correspondence, and also the infamous *Essay on the Noble Science of Self-Justification*. This collection was first published in 1795 and at the time was considered to be a humorous contribution to the debate on the education of women.

Every issue of *Lady of the House* featured a '*Lady of the House* Forum of Debate'. In the January 1909 edition, readers were informed:

Skirts will be worn short. The rinking craze, and the opening of the golf season will make this single style sensible and desirable, and it is especially suitable for wear in our exceptionally muddy streets.

Practicality had become a consideration in clothing as the Edwardian era brought with it a more egalitarian approach to design. Men across the social spectrum began wearing similarly designed shirts and collars. To a certain degree this approach was replicated in women's fashion but there were more radical changes taking place beneath their skirts. Underwear had become attractive and was no longer strictly functional. Although expensive corsets had already been available in a range of colours the Edwardian era saw a radical change in underwear across the board. Not only did it shape and enhance the figure, it titillated and aroused those lucky enough to see it up close.

Whether Anna Haslam was wearing petticoats decorated with satin ribbons or a sleeveless chemise we cannot be sure, but perhaps when setting out to attend the meetings of the first suffrage society in Dublin she considered the length of her petticoat and selected one with a shorter skirt to ensure it would not trail along the muddy streets.

The IWSLGA were strictly non-militant, their campaigns never breached the letter of the law and they achieved their goals through endless petitioning to the government in Westminster. They frequently wrote letters to the press and various heads of state. In the IWSLGA annual report it was proudly noted that twenty-seven petitions in 1886 and seventeen in 1890 had been sent to the House of Commons.

By the beginning of the twentieth century Irish women who fulfilled certain property ownership criteria could serve as poor-law guardians and vote in Local Government elections despite the well publicised fears of some House of Commons MPs who were convinced that this new 'petticoat government' would lead to no good.

Edwardian petticoats were traditionally quite flimsy and rarely more than two layers were worn at any time but by the late 1910s, fashion had dictated that petticoats had more frills or 'frou frou' as it was sometimes known and the borders were often stiffened with horse hair or steel to maintain their flounce and shape. Perhaps if those rambunctious MPs had cared to try on a petticoat for themselves they might have concluded that the world was quite safe from female domination given the weight and restrictive nature of the yards of heavy material.

In 1905 the Gibson Girl, a popular illustration by American artist, Charles Dana Gibson, which appeared in a number of fashion magazines and novels, epitomised the ideal shape. The corset had become shorter above the waist and longer below stretching down over the hips. The skirt was narrow for the most part but dissolved gradually into a whirlpool of petticoat at the feet. The corset no longer focused on sculpting the waist and chest but was designed to incorporate the hips and thighs and although physical movement was impaired, the chest and lungs were permitted more freedom than previous fashions had allowed. So even though the women of the IWSLGA were not clamouring over the gates of government or demonstrating in the streets, their lung capacity was no longer diminished by their stays and as history has told us, their voices were eventually heard.

Deeds Not Words!

Across the Irish Sea a Manchester-based suffrage campaigner named Emmeline Pankhurst had become disillusioned by the women's movement which was led largely by the National Union of Women's Suffrage Societies. Pankhurst and her two daughters, Christabel and Sylvia, opted to set up their own society, the Women's Social and Political Union (WSPU).

The WSPU set their sights on greater equality in various areas of employment and society. Unlike their predecessors, they took a more militant approach from the outset. The WSPU considered the mainstream women's movement ceremonial and ineffective and before long they had identified the electoral vote as the key to equality. The members favoured a wide range of non-traditional, attention-seeking tactics that became known as suffrage militancy.

In 1907, Emmeline Pankhurst gave up her fulltime employment and moved the headquarters of the WSPU to London. The WSPU motto was 'Deeds not Words!' and members consistently rejected discussion, compromise and slow progress in favour of symbolic action that demanded attention.

Activists chained themselves to the railings of the British parliament buildings to raise public awareness of their cause. They were very often arrested and imprisoned and it was during these periods of incarceration that Pankhurst and many of her followers went on hunger-strike. It wasn't long before the *Daily Mail* newspaper had nick-named Pankhurst and the WSPU 'the suffragettes'.

> We women of a younger generation are in somewhat of a hurry for reform

Pankhurst believed strongly in the importance of passion over reason and in the ability of individuals to bring about dramatic change through spiritual greatness. Joan of Arc was adopted as their heroine and she became a familiar image on the WSPU posters: numerous marches were led by women dressed in her image, wearing armour and riding on white horses. Undoubtedly Emmeline and her fellow suffragettes were wearing their usual underwear but it is hard to imagine they opted for horsehair petticoats underneath their clothing. Dressing for battle inevitably led to a reduction in the heavy artillery beneath.

Meanwhile the first raft of formally educated women had graduated from universities in Ireland and, tired of the punctiliousness of the IWSLGA, they too were anxious for radical change. Fired up by reports of suffragist activists on hunger-strike and serving prison sentences in England, the Irish Women's Franchise League was formed in 1908, led by Hanna Sheehy Skeffington.

Unlike Anna Haslam and the IWSLGA, they were resolved to go to any lengths to secure the parliamentary vote for Irish women. The Irish Women's Franchise League was avowedly militant in pursuit of their goal. They had become impatient with the polite letters of the IWSLGA and were determined to create a stir. They staged protests and held regular meetings in Phoenix Park where speakers were subjected to verbal abuse and very often assaulted with rotten eggs and over-ripe tomatoes. In June 1912, eight members of the Irish Women's Franchise League were arrested for breaking the windows of the government buildings in Dublin. When they refused to pay their fines they were convicted by the courts for their activities. On the eve of her imprisonment, Hannah Sheehy Skeffington wrote:

We women of a younger generation are somewhat in a hurry with reform.

A number of years later, Hannah Sheehy Skeffington was encouraged to write about her experiences and in between reminiscences of soapbox speeches and prison food, she admitted that in the midst of all their militant activities, the IWFL were not averse to utilising their feminine wiles:

In 1912 we went to Mountjoy Jail, six of us. That year a weekly paper founded and edited by James Cousins and Francis Skeffington was launched; we had arrived! Our paper was shortly on sale at all meetings, in the street. We had colours (orange and green), a Vote for Women badge, slogans; we made use, with genuine ingenuity, of many good publicity devices

and stunts and became a picturesque element in Irish life, the Irish being always glad of any
new element, especially one that challenged and took sides.

They may have been dodging tomatoes but they were still aware of their 'picturesque' presence. Similarly, Emmeline Pankhurst was always careful to place the best-looking suffragists at the front of their marches in an attempt to woo the British newspaper photographers.

Despite the support from some sections of Irish society, just like the English 'suffragettes', Hannah Sheehy Skeffington did not have support from women across the board. They were vilified for what was perceived as unfeminine and vulgar politics and chastised for turning their backs on more womanly duties. In the discussion pages of *Lady of the House* in March 1909, the topic for debate was 'Is Today's Woman Good To Her Menfolk?'

One correspondent, Miss I. V. McComas from Merrion Road, Dublin, publicly distanced herself from the 'suffragettes' and declared that a woman's rightful and instinctive duty was to ensure the happiness of her husband and family:

The Suffragettes may 'go forth to war' but deep in every true woman's heart will I believe,
always burn that fire of love, Divinely lighted, which makes home her best place: and her
children, husband, loved ones, her first and greatest love ... I think the woman of today is
as good to her menfolk as ever she has been in times past. With this difference, that whereas
formerly she was content to see after their bodily comforts only, to stay at home – the house
drudge – now she goes further – joins in their amusements, interests herself in their occupa-
tions, and is, in fact, their companion as well as their housekeeper.

So while women like Anna Haslam, Isabella Todd and Hannah Sheehy Skeffington were galvanising women to campaign for their right to vote, their efforts were considered unwomanly. The modern young woman had to be careful of the toes she might be treading on. While it was unacceptable to seek equality in the ballot box, the same issue of the magazine heralded the new ground broken by a young Irish woman in London: 'Sheila O'Neill' was featured as a news item in their social affairs section due to her success as the first lady cab driver in London:

> The march of science may bring us many stranger and new things with it, and not the least strange to our old fashioned ideas is the lady chauffeur, and yet there does not seem to be any good reason why a woman should not be successful in the role, requiring, as it does, quickness of eye, neatness of hand, and general adaptability, all of which are fairly common characteristics … Miss Sheila O'Neill (who, from her name, we may surely hail as a fellow countrywoman) is following it in London with pleasure and profit, and has the distinction of being the first of her sex to appear in the capacity in that city. She has been out, we are told, nearly everyday, and has been so successful that her employer has received a number of applications from young women who desire to follow Miss O'Neill's example and become motor car drivers. Her 'fares' have found her driving quite as satisfactory as that of men drivers.

Sheila O'Neill's feminine daintiness and 'neatness of hand' had assured her success behind the wheel and the support of her establishment sisters at home.

The only women to command respect as political figures in Ireland were those who dedicated their efforts to Irish nationalism and liberation from British rule.

Countess Constance Markiewicz, a heroine of Irish nationalist politics, first became involved in the fight for independence when she attended a meeting of Inghinidhe na hÉireann (Daughters of Ireland): an association established by Maud Gonne in 1900, dedicated to the independence of Ireland and fostering an appreciation of Irish language and culture among women.

There are various sensational accounts of her arrival upon the Irish political scene. Many writers have recalled how she swept into a Inghinidhe na hÉireann meeting bedecked in jewellery and wearing a flowing ballgown having attended a dinner function at Dublin Castle, the seat of British rule in Ireland. Her fellow 'daughters' were suspicious of her motives initially because of her social position and wealth but it didn't take long for Constance to win them over with her intellect and charm. Soon after her first meeting she advised them all to 'leave your jewels and wands in the bank and go out and buy a revolver'.

Constance Markiewicz was a woman renowned for her spirited personality. She later went on to establish Fianna Éireann in 1909 and served as second-in-command in the Irish Citizen Army during the 1916 Rising. In 1918, as a Sinn Féin candidate, she became the first woman elected to the British House of Commons.

Women's right to vote was finally enshrined in the Irish constitution in 1922, six years before their female counterparts in Britain. But despite the political and social position of women like Constance Markiewicz and Maud Gonne, their voices were raised for their country and not for women. The only independence they fought for was that of Ireland, any thoughts of their own emancipation were considered a distraction from the more important nationalist cause. Members of women's groups such as Cumann na mBan, which formed in April 1914 with the sole purpose of providing support to the all-male Irish Volunteers, placed the independence of Ireland before their own.

Bright Young Things

The invention of the 'flapper' was that descended across much of aftermath of the First World new breath of life, the boom in industry, aviation, nication. The world was than ever before.

> " Women have taken a very large step towards nudity, and sex appeal has vanished. "

the perfect antidote to the gloom Europe and America in the War. A new decade and a Roaring Twenties led to a motor cars and commu- changing at a faster pace

In the midst of all this as a physical manifestation of vitality. She danced the Charleston, change the 'flapper' evolved this sudden surge of youth and dared to wear her skirts shorter and even bobbed her hair. A new demographic had emerged between childhood and marriage: the bright young thing determined to embrace life and all the newfound liberties provided by the suffragist movement.

The fashion industry reflected this era with an exciting new look: hemlines were raised higher than ever before, waistlines were dropped and the traditional cinched waist or pushed-up bosom was replaced with a revolutionary boyish silhouette. Women no longer wanted to dress like younger versions of their mothers and grandmothers. For the first time in history they had a look that was entirely their own.

Naturally underwear designers had to respond to these seismic changes and design suitable lingerie. The working, voting and Charleston-dancing gal about town certainly couldn't navigate the streets and dance floors constrained by her corset.

This particular period has also been identified as the dawn of 'nudity' – albeit extremely limited by today's standards. Evening-wear had always permitted women to display their bare arms and décolletage but the expanse of flesh revealed by the latest fashions was new ground indeed.

Fashion historians and writers have proffered many explanations for this sudden and dramatic change in fashion. Alison Lurie writes in *The Language of Clothes* that this new love affair with the flesh was a subconscious attempt to encourage procreation after the loss of life in the First World War. Others have suggested that it was a bid to promote equality across the social spectrum and what better territory upon which to execute this than the skin itself?

Women began to oil their bodies with cosmetic products previously unavailable to the mass market and for the first time in modern history, bronzed skin became fashionable. For centuries tanning was an indication of poverty and low social standing as only those who were forced to work in the open air could suffer a tan. In the 1920s the reverse became the case: as the increase in industry drew manual workers indoors the wealthy elite chose to holiday along the coastline of the Mediterranean. Their bronzed bodies replaced their diamonds and frippery as a sign of wealth and position.

Naturally such innovations were met with a certain level of opposition. There is a recording of Maud Gonne addressing a gathering of the Daughters of Éireann where she criticised the latest fashions:

Irish girls, do not become flappers. Do your work for your country, serve her as tastefully and your own lives become more excitingly interested [sic].

Nor was playwright George Bernard Shaw in favour of this new interest in the flesh. Known for his dry wit and acerbic social commentary, in 1929 he made short shrift of this new trend in women's fashions:

Women have taken a very large step towards nudity, and sex appeal has vanished. Bring back clothes and it would be increased.

Irish attitudes towards dress and morality were more traditional as illustrated by the audience reaction to the first production of J. M. Synge's *Playboy of the Western World* in the Abbey Theatre in 1909. During the course of the play one of the characters makes reference to women in their 'shifts' – a term used for a slip or a chemise – and the audience was sent into uproar because the playwright had dared to mention women's underwear in public. On the first night Lady Gregory telegraphed after Act One to the absent W. B. Yeats, a co-founder of the National Theatre:

Play great success.

Ten minutes before the end, however, the growing disquiet among the audience had turned into riot, prompting her to transmit the notorious missive:

Audience broke up in disorder after the word 'shift'.

Despite the new fashion for svelte, curveless physiques, the traditional cumbersome corset was still worn by ladies of an older generation. Younger women opted for longer vest-like corsetry that did not gather at the waist but rather focused upon diminishing the chest by flattening the bosom. They wore girdles which compressed the hips providing the much sought-after nubile and lithe figure synonymous with this new era of exploration and discovery.

Although women were still contorting their natural shape, their undergarments permitted a greater degree of movement than the Edwardian corset. Women had begun to move in spheres previously confined to men, and their underwear, their support structure, had to travel with them.

An Independent Woman

In the years following the War of Independence in Ireland, the Church and State were eager to forge an identity for Ireland far removed from that of its former British occupier. The leaders of the new republic concluded in these changing times that the Irish family was under threat. Women, who had been actively involved in the struggle for independence, had enjoyed a greater degree of freedom and movement than that of their ancestors. Furthermore, the influence of British culture and the radically changing fashions had produced a young and vibrant generation that the newly-formed Republic of Ireland was determined to rein in.

As women took up their recently-obtained electoral vote and a new generation of young educated women began considering their options, the Church and State colluded to curb, if not completely strangle, the blossoming independent Irish woman.

From the mid 1920s onwards, the new Irish government introduced various pieces of legislation which curtailed the employment of married women in the civil service and the teaching profession. In 1935, the government assumed the right to limit the employment of women in any given industry and, in 1937, the constitution defined the role of women, particularly mothers, living in the state, exclusively in terms of family and the home:

1. In particular the State recognises that by her life within the home, woman gives to the State a support without which the common good cannot be achieved.

2. The State shall therefore, endeavour to ensure that mothers shall not be obliged by the economic necessity to engage in labour to the neglect of their duties in the home.

(Article 41.2)

There were eleven female representatives elected to the houses of the oireachtas between 1922 and 1937.

Bridget Redmond and Mary Reynolds, both members of Cumann na nGaedheal, were elected in by-elections following the death of their husbands. Similarly, Margaret Collins O'Driscoll succeeded her brother, Cumann na nGaedheal leader, Michael Collins. These women seldom contributed to debate during a period when a series of reforms restricting women's social position were passed through the dáil. Their subdued performance is perhaps due to the fact that they were elected on the basis of their family connection as opposed to any political beliefs they may have had. They were perceived as symbolic figureheads for the party they represented; they were seen and not heard.

Loose Women

In addition to the new state restrictions on the employment of married women, the Catholic Church set about terrifying their congregations with threats of hell and damnation should loose morals and hedonistic pursuits be entertained in good god-fearing homes.

Women and their morality had become a barometer for Irish national identity. They were a symbol of all that was true and virtuous in the brave new Ireland yet simultaneously their bodies had the potential to cause total disruption to society. The stereotypical 'flapper' of the 1920s was considered the living embodiment of all that was threatening to the Irish Catholic ideal.

In the March 1927 editorial of the *Irish Catholic*, a monthly publication, the editor warned of the dangerous 'lure of exotic dances, extravagance and immodesty in dress, and the craze for hectic pleasure of every kind'. Such pursuits were considered reckless and were associated with the culture of the state's former occupiers.

Many historians have argued that the legislative restrictions and ecclesiastical threats of eternal damnation for all women who dared to step outside the virtuous, god-fearing domestic shell were due to her refusal to conform to their vision of womanhood.

Dr Maryann Valiulis, author of an essay entitled 'Neither Feminist Nor Flapper' suggests this ecclesiastical determination to restrict women's independence was, in part, a response to the changes of a modernising society. It was among women that modernisation and cultural change were most visible: they began to work, bob their hair, dance and, most importantly, they continued to emigrate in droves.

The War and the Waspie

By the 1940s, magazine fashion editors began declaring 'there is no such thing as a stylish stout', according to writer Caroline Cox in *Lingerie, A Lexicon of Style*. Women were no longer encouraged to rely solely on their corsets to provide the shape they desired and magazines frequently suggested a range of exercises and diets as a form of body manipulation.

During the Second World War, women's contribution to industry demanded they actively engage in labour and the boned stomach-flattening girdles were phased out in favour of lastex or elasticised models nick-named 'roll-ons', famously developed by the Dunlop Rubber Company.

Although Ireland remained neutral throughout the Second World War, the subsequent shortages experienced in the UK also took their toll in Ireland. The 'Special Period', as it became known, was characterised by a scarcity of goods previously in plentiful supply, including fabrics for clothing and underwear.

Elsewhere in Europe, the layers of chemise, vest and petticoat became cumbersome for women busily filling the shoes of the absent menfolk and, in light of the international shortages, such decadent trappings were considered indulgent. Furthermore, practicality had become a serious issue, the hemline was raised ever so slightly and this time it was not to dance the Charleston but to work for their country unhindered.

In the years following the war, Paris was determined to return to its former elegance and sophistication. Although much of the city's art had been looted and buildings destroyed during the conflict, the fashion industry had weathered the storm. Designers such as Balenciaga and Schiaperelli had managed to hold on to their ateliers during the Nazi occupation but despite their fortitude there was only one designer who succeeded in translating the post-war exuberance into his collection: Christian Dior.

> **There is no such thing as a stylish stout.**

In 1947, Dior presented the Carolle line or 'New Look' as it became known. He was hailed as a genius and his collection a masterpiece, the sleek lines of the late 1930s and early 1940s were abandoned in favour of cinched and bell-shaped skirts. Dior's New Look was a breath of fresh air after the bleak years of conflict. His new silhouette was seen as a determined about-turn from the war-induced deprivation; the Carolle line was probably the most influential of his career.

The New Look became synonymous with the Parisian determination to restore life and vitality to their post-war capital. Instead of the narrow skirts which had dominated fashion throughout the war years, Dior created wide, flowing skirts made from copious amounts of sumptuous fabric. The new shape was considered ultra-feminine, the tiny-waisted figure was delicate and fragile. The war was over and women no longer needed to dress for practicality.

Many fashion writers have compared the 'waist-cincher' girdles which accompanied Dior's New Look with the narrow-waisted shape fashionable throughout much of the nineteenth century. Although the fashion industry heralded the Christian Dior collection as the most exciting the world had seen in decades, there were certain sections of society which resented this return to restrictive clothing.

In *Lingerie, a Lexicon of Style,* Caroline Cox makes reference to an article which appeared in the magazine, *Picture Post,* which described the new trend as wholly impractical for the working woman:

> *Paris forgets this is 1947. There can be no question about the entire unsuitability of these new fashions for our present life and times. Think of doing housework, or sitting at a typewriter all day, or working in a factory, tightly corseted and encumbered and constricted with layers of hip padding and petticoats. Our mothers freed us from these in their struggle for emancipation and in our own active, workaday lives there can be no place for them.*

Picture Post captured the frustrations felt by women throughout Europe who, just a few years previously, had been called upon to leave their homes and make a vital contribution to the war effort. Following the end of conflict and the return of the menfolk, many women objected to the presumption they would simply hang up their tools, bind their waists and return to their domestic chores.

In Ireland, women were still trying to take advantage of the limited freedoms afforded to them by the ever more patriarchal culture. Despite the rebellious spirit evidenced in their determination to emigrate, work and even just enjoy life, the law of the land afforded few liberties and ensured they remained dependent upon their husbands, fathers and brothers for long-term financial security.

By the late 1950s, contraception was effectively illegal as it was an offence to sell or import any form of contraceptives. Women employed in public service and a high proportion of other industries were ordered to relinquish their careers as soon as they married.

As the twentieth century passed its halfway point, it seemed as if the waists and careers of Irish women were as restricted as those of their great-grandmothers.

Post-Pill Paradise

Just over a decade later and the lives of women all over the world were to change forever following the introduction of the contraceptive pill.

The pill was a revolution for women who for the first time could exert control over their fertility and, by direct consequence, their entire lives. Unsurprisingly, the Catholic Church condemned such developments and priests harangued their god-fearing parishioners with threats of hellfire should any man or woman attempt to interfere with nature.

Although it would seem that Ireland was heaping repression upon women by preventing access to contraception, Irish men and women were undeterred. Family Planning clinics opened in Dublin and while the pill could not be prescribed for contraception many doctors circumvented the law by providing it as a means of regulating a woman's menstrual cycle. Naturally many women were only too willing to exploit these well-publicised 'side-effects'.

The streets of Dublin and Cork may not have shared the atmosphere of London and New York, where the sexual revolution was in full swing, but sex was still gradually becoming something not to be ashamed of. Unplanned pregnancies could be prevented and the repercussions of sex were no longer seen as mostly negative.

Accompanying this dramatic change in attitude came a completely new shape. The hour-glass figure that had dominated so much of the 1940s and 1950s was replaced with a boyish, lean figure wrapped in mini-skirts and draped in A-line shift dresses.

> **The lives of women were to change forever following the introduction of the pill**

This androgynous look, similar to the flapper silhouette which emerged during the 1920s, reflected the rebellious spirit of a young generation determined to break the mould. Clothes were more free-moving than they had ever been, legs stretched un-inhibited under mini-skirts and trousers, breathing was not restricted by girdles and sturdy brassieres, and the ideal shape underneath these new fashions was thin and waif-like.

Underwear offered less control and more freedom and comfort than it had ever done before. The English model Twiggy, her nickname derived from her incredibly thin frame, became the face synonymous with the decade. Her staring eyes gazed out of a child-like face and her matchstick arms and legs branched out from under her flimsy shift dress; her body was so small and fragile she had little to support or contain.

Despite the newfound sexual liberty in what American novelist John Updike called 'the post-pill paradise', women in Ireland and across the world were still not on equal footing with men socially, economically or legally. The fashionable figure of the waif, with all her boy-child charm, was a reflection of their marginalised position.

For the previous sixty years women had campaigned, lobbied, suffered imprisonment and voluntarily starved themselves in a bid to be recognised as equal citizens and yet, although they had come a certain distance, they still had a long way to travel.

Braless and Brazen

Throughout the 1960s, the feminist movement had been gathering steam and, by the early 1970s, it had emerged kicking and screaming. Across the UK, Ireland and the United States women were taking to the streets, demanding equal rights across the board.

For some, the feminist movement became synonymous with all that was distinctly unfeminine. Sections of the media particularly feasted upon this image and went to great lengths to portray leaders of the movement as unwomanly and therefore inhuman. This in turn successfully transformed women's campaign for equality into an altogether more threatening vista: a campaign for changes which, if implemented, would damage society as a whole.

A prime example of the media's ability to confuse and distort events took place in 1968 when feminists were reported by the press as symbolically burning their bras in the streets. Fashion writer Caroline Cox suggests this did not occur but was in fact the result of an error on the part of a few journalists. A group of American women who called themselves the 'New York Radical Women' had gathered in Atlantic City to protest against the Miss America pageant and had ceremoniously dumped their brassieres in trash cans. Simultaneously in New York anti-war protesters were burning their Vietnam draft cards. The newspapers confused the two events.

The bra-burning association has remained and the extremist image it conjures has perpetually been used to devalue the feminist movement. The brassiere and all its variations has been supporting women's bodies for centuries so to discard and destroy it indicates an absence of rationale. This is how mainstream media have portrayed feminism — as a set of demands promoted by irrational and uncompromising women. The more extremist and 'unwomanly' they appeared, the easier they were to dismiss.

The Irish Women's Liberation Movement formed in 1970 and a year later they presented their manifesto, 'Chains or Change', on *The Late Late Show*, a popular prime time Irish television programme. They had five demands: equal pay, equal education, equality before the law, contraception, and justice for deserted wives, unmarried mothers and widows.

Among the movement, there were a number of journalists who successfully disseminated the message to the public via the media. Women's rights became an issue, a topic of conversation on the airwaves and on television and, in response to this, national newspapers began to include sections devoted wholly to women's issues. The *Irish Times* established its 'Women First' pages in the early 1970s and they became a vital forum for debate. Although they often included articles on fashion and cookery, issues such as employment equality, contraception and abortion were also discussed.

Author Nell McCafferty, a well-known journalist for the *Irish Times* and later *The Sunday Tribune*, was an outspoken member of the Women's Liberation Movement. In 1971, she and almost fifty other members of the movement, including Mary Kenny and June Levine, took the train to Belfast. Their mission was to purchase condoms and the contraceptive pill with the intention of bringing them back into the Republic of Ireland. It was a symbolic journey and was the focus of public debate in the days and weeks following (despite the fact that the women returned flourishing aspirin 'pills' and not the desired 'pill' because they had not realised a doctor's prescription was required).

> **The media portrayed feminism as a set of demands promoted by irrational women**

By the mid 1970s the feminist debate was no longer confined to the columns of women's pages and in August 1974, the issue of public bathing in south Dublin sparked a remarkable level of debate.

The Forty Foot, a picturesque section of the coast in south Dublin, was restricted to men only and up until 9 a.m. the gentlemen swimmers could cut through the waves unencumbered by their togs as 'nude bathing' was extremely popular. That August was particularly temperate and members of the women's movement objected that such a nice section of the coastline was out of bounds. For four consecutive weekends, media from all over the world watched as these emboldened bathers traversed the barrier and swam alongside the men.

The militant bathers were supported in some corners but the subsequent reporting by the media was particularly damaging and prompted *Irish Times* columnist Christina Murphy to write:

Quite frankly I think the whole thing is a waste of time and a red herring as far as the real issue of women's liberation is concerned. It has managed to confirm a lot of men in what they always thought about women's liberation (and which is not true): that those involved are irresponsible, publicity-seeking sensationalists. And I have an awful feeling that it is going to acquire the status of bra-burning in the folklore of the Irish women's movement.

Agitation and Amendments

In 1970 there were seventeen associations devoted to promoting the rights of women in Ireland. By 1980 there were almost sixty, a substantial proportion of which were government-funded. The women's movement had been active for ten years and, although they had not yet achieved all they had set out to do, the Irish government's willingness to fund their organisations was an indication that they were making an impact.

Elsewhere, the feminist movement continued apace; Margaret Thatcher had earned her moniker as the 'Iron Lady' as Britain's first female prime minister and contraception, anti-discrimination laws and the right to abortion were introduced in the UK and throughout a number of European countries. Meanwhile Ireland seemed to be lagging behind: the economic recession had led many young people to emigrate and the Catholic Church was a dominating force, particularly in rural areas. Divorce was still not an option for unhappy couples and while contraception had been legalised, it was only available on a limited basis from GPs and Family Planning clinics.

Ireland's membership of the EU resulted in various forms of European anti-discrimination and employment legislation being absorbed into the Irish system. Change was gradually taking place. When these developments are put in the context of the position of women in the years immediately following the establishment of the Irish Republic, women had come a long way.

All this change was brought about with or without the brassiere because by the mid to late 1980s underwear was no longer an all-important foundation layer of every woman's wardrobe – it was now a matter of choice. Hygiene, warmth and shape, the functions demanded of underwear in the past, seemed irrelevant in modern society. When a woman made her underwear selection it could be for any number of reasons; it was her choice and her choice alone.

Similarly, underwear was just as attractive in its absence, most notably immortalised on the silver screen by Sharon Stone in *Basic Instinct* when, playing the role of the blonde seductress, she uncrossed and crossed her legs to reveal that less was definitely more.

Modern Woman

In recent years underwear has been given a new responsibility: it has become a must-have luxury item to be worn by women determined to make an impression in the bedroom and on their bank balances. Designers such as La Perla, Strumpet and Pink, and Agent Provocateur have designed reassuringly expensive lingerie which is a cut above the underwear produced by celebrity-endorsed brands and de-partment stores.

Agent Provocateur, created by Joseph Corre (son of Vivienne Westwood) and Serena Rees, design underwear which is not so much worn as exhibited. Their lingerie is for women who wear their underwear on the outside and their sexuality on their sleeve. They design underwear which is both exclu-sive enough for Hollywood movie stars and almost essential for the twenty- first century woman. As they say on their website:

> "Exclusive underwear is now aspirational as it promises enhanced power and self-esteem"

A woman wearing a scrumptious pair of turquoise tulle knickers promotes in herself a sexy superhero feeling which exudes itself as a confident and positive sexuality.

Lingerie design labels have created their own brand hierarchy similar to that of expensive clothes, watches and cars. Exclusive underwear is now aspirational as it promises enhanced power and self-esteem. One hundred years ago stays and whalebone were used to create the ideal physical shape, today's underwear is more about a psychological shaping-up. It seems as if the modern women is in as much need of support as her ancestors.

Chapter Four
Culture

Some women are known for their clothes and some for their underwear. Most women keep their smalls under wraps while others have made their name, fortune and sometimes even history as a result of their underwear.

American Jazz performer Josephine Baker wore little more than a belt of bananas when she danced at the Folie Bergères in Paris during the 1920s. One of the most iconic images of Marilyn Monroe is taken from the film, *The Seven Year Itch,* when her skirt billows up around her waist revealing her girdle-less thighs and white knickers. Princess Diana delighted her adoring fans when she admitted to wearing thermal underwear underneath her evening gowns so that she could stand still in draughty halls without catching pneumonia. Monica Lewinsky graduated from being a White House intern to an international household name when it emerged that she had conducted an affair with Bill Clinton. As the scandal unravelled, it transpired that her preferred style of underwear – the thong – was also a favourite with the US president.

In addition to being a reflection of fashion and the style of the individual woman wearing it, underwear can also serve as a cultural landmark of the society in which it was first manufactured.

The label on a piece of underwear reveals not only the size of the owner and where she made her purchase but the design, structure, colour and material can provide an up close and personal insight into the wearer. Whether it's Marks and Spencer multi-pack white garters, sport bras or silk bottom-cleavage knickers from Strumpet and Pink, the underwear in your shopping basket says something about you and the world you live in.

Given the 'wardrobe DNA' one can harvest from an underwear label, to what extent does underwear reflect women and their lives? Could it be described as a second skin? Does it camouflage or coerce? Is underwear chosen by women or chosen for them by the society they inhabit?

Health Hazard

'Burn the corsets!' wrote the feminist writer Elizabeth Stuart Phelps in 1874. 'Make a bonfire of the cruel steels that have lorded it over your thorax and abdomen and heave a sigh of relief.'

One hundred years ago women were repeatedly warned about the damage their underwear was doing to their health. Fashion prescribed small waists and narrow hips but women were regularly warned by medical journals, periodicals and a limited number of outspoken female voices about the dangers of tight-lacing. Newspapers and magazines reported endless tales of corset-induced maladies, which ranged from feelings of faintness to skin abrasions and even miscarriage. Nevertheless the clothing industry still continued to design and make clothing that required a certain amount of cinching before the wearer could get dressed.

In the 1939 movie version of Margaret Mitchell's novel, *Gone With the Wind*, the vivacious Scarlett O'Hara, played by Vivien Leigh, is admonished by her maid 'Mammy' for insisting that her stays be tied tighter. In one of the opening scenes of the film, Scarlett determinedly grips the bedpost while Mammy, played by Hattie McDaniel, battles with her corset from behind.

Women who favoured 'tight-lacing' have invariably been considered vampish and even immoral. Early pornographic images often featured women wearing extremely narrow corsets as though to emphasise an innate sexual energy that required stringent restriction.

Dr Gustave Jaeger established his clothing business on the basis of his belief that because his woollens were undyed and therefore 'natural' they were more capable of distributing bodily toxins, and enabled the skin to breathe more freely. He considered vegetable products such as cotton and linen (or as he described 'the insect excretion known as silk') to be contaminated by treatment and, as a result, unhealthy. Jaeger's designs were directed more at men although he often stressed the dangers associated with women's heavy underclothes. He regularly preached the benefits of exercise as a means of promoting his clothes, particularly his bathing suits, and made reference to the number of drowning accidents caused by restrictive clothing:

The more general use of the Jaeger swimming dress at our sea-side resorts, would no doubt tend to diminish greatly the number of bathing fatalities which fill the columns of newspapers during the holiday season, and are so frequently the result of sudden cramp and impaired action of the heart, caused by the diminution of animal heat, against which the unclothed swimmer, however skilful, has no defence.

By the turn of the century, the grumbling of the bohemian avant-garde gained more general acceptance. Advertisers began promoting women's underwear as garments that provided 'comfort'; the shape-giving attributes being but an added bonus. Manufacturers at the beginning of the twentieth century felt they had to concede that a woman's underwear might be for her own personal benefit.

This promotion of fashion, comfort and also economy showed the influence of the Rational Dress movement. It originated during the Victorian era as a fleeting obsession among the more bohemian elements of society but by the early 1910s the fashion industry had begun to listen and respond.

French designer Paul Poiret had been plucked from his position as delivery boy at an umbrella manufacturer and installed in the highly respected Maison Worth in Paris. Maison Worth was an established couture house, run by two brothers, Gaston and Jean-Phillipe, who had inherited the business from their father, the famous Edwardian designer, Charles Frederick Worth. They realised that in order to maintain their position at the top of the Parisian fashion industry they needed to appeal to the younger woman.

Poiret's contribution to Maison Worth was considered to be impressive and it established him as one of Paris' brightest new talents, however, due to artistic differences the association lasted only two years and Poiret left Maison Worth and began working for Jacques Doucet. His marriage to Denise Boulet in 1905, the daughter of a provincial textile manufacturer, provided him with an ideal muse. According to fashion historian Christopher Breward, it was largely due to her vivacious personality and Poiret's ability to generate publicity that he succeeded in delivering one of his most notable collections in 1907: the Directoire line.

British fashion designer Matthew Williamson has a certain amount in common with Paul Poiret as both men made their name from creating flamboyant and directional evening-wear for the rich and famous. Poiret made a point of hosting numerous high profile soirées during which carefully selected society ladies would be dressed in the designer's latest creations. Similarly Williamson has carved his niche dress- ing the latest bright young things in the world of fashion and film such as Jade Jagger and, more recently, actress Sienna Miller.

The empire lines and soft silhouettes which characte- rised Poiret's dresses were intended to mark a libera- tion of the female body and a radical departure from the long-held belief that physical beauty was inter- twined with curves created by lacing and padding. While Poiret was perhaps renowned for his new perspective on shape he had, in fact, capitalised on a slow-moving trend that a handful of designers had been working on for almost a decade.

> **The demand for more discreet underwear was by no means an indication of a more prudish society**

Apart from the small number of extremist voices that demanded corsetry be burned at the stake however, most women regarded their corsets as essential for their shape and beneficial to their health, wellbeing and sense of propriety. The corset was worn not only by women but also by children in the belief that it improved posture and alignment. While the bodices worn by young boys and girls were not nearly as restrictive as a full-blown corset, they were nonetheless considered an essential piece of daily attire without which the body would be in danger of roaming unsupported. In fact, well-to-do men also wore a form of corsetry during the nineteenth and early twentieth century to accentuate the breadth of the chest by drawing in the waist beneath.

During this period, it was generally acknowledged that shape was achieved by underclothes. This was to change dramatically by the mid 1920s and 1930s when the fashion world began stripping away layers of clothing forcing underwear to become more discreet and subtle in its manipulation of the female form.

Flapper Fashions

No sooner had Europe redrawn its borders following the First World War, than the fashion industry also began exploring new territory: the skin. As business and industry began to flourish across America and Europe, women started to discard layers of clothing; never before had so much flesh been on display.

The new boyish silhouette created notions of ease and effortless style but getting the desired shape was still an issue. Underwear continued to play a vital role, strapping down chests and slimming hips but under no circumstances was this work to be acknowledged in public. Underwear was now only to be seen by the wearer and her chosen audience; it was by no means intended for display.

The women of the 1920s occupied a better position politically and socially than they had done for centuries. While their waists were no longer under the tight grip of stays and whalebone, fashionable society had placed an additional onus upon their bodies; not only should they endeavour to become a certain shape but it had to appear natural! While their domestically-bound mothers and grandmothers before them made no apology for their underwear, the 'Bright Young Things' a few decades later were expected to keep their shape-inducing prowess strictly private.

This demand for discreet underwear was not an indication of a more prudish society, it was in fact quite the opposite: the growth of the film industry and its accompanying starlets had discovered sex to be a lucrative selling ploy. Fashion followed suit and clothes became more tight-fitting and revealing, it was only the underwear that remained under wraps.

Elastic Fantastic

The fashion for body-shaping dresses needed a new style of underwear and by this time the lingerie industry had discovered rubber, thereby creating a revolution in women's underwear. The Dunlop Rubber Company's research had discovered a treatment which transformed the raw latex solution imported from the Far East into a strong elastic thread that could be produced in a variety of widths and thicknesses. Lastex was born and underwear was transformed overnight; thick corsets and girdles became a thing of the past. The new fabric was ideal for creating shape in secret.

In 1925 the American company Gossard launched a new line in 'corsellettes' called the 'Gossard Complete' with the tag-line 'On in 17 seconds'. It's hard to imagine this being a selling point but in comparison to the underclothes of previous generations, the 'Gossard Complete' was a welcome arrival. Not only was it slim-fitting and therefore inconspicuous, it was side-fastening – a woman could put it on and take it off without assistance. It was also low-backed and therefore ideal for wearing under evening gowns. Similarly, the 'roll-on' corset, first introduced in the 1930s, was a relatively subtle garment which remained popular among women until the mid 1960s.

Elsa Schiaperelli created the most sensational dresses of the 1930s during her collaboration with Surrealist artist Salvador Dali. Two of her most famous pieces, one entitled The Tear, and the other, The Lobster – worn by New York socialite and soon-to-be Duchess of Windsor, Mrs Wallis Simpson – created a stir when they emerged in 1938. Simpson, who famously remarked that one could 'Never be too rich or too thin', was a woman who made good use of the latest and most discreet underwear.

Dali designed the pattern of the fabric and Schiaperelli designed the dress itself. The Lobster Dress was inspired by two of Dali's most famous pieces, *New York Dream – Man Finds Lobster in Place of Phone* (1935) and *Lobster Telephone* (1936). The lobster always had strong sexual connotations for Dali but when his vivid lobsters were sensuously hugging the thighs of Mrs Wallis Simpson, the look was charged with erotic tension.

Schiaperelli had earned a reputation for her thought-provoking designs and in 1932 *The New Yorker* magazine wrote: 'A frock from Schiaperelli ranks like a modern canvas.' No dress embodied this sentiment more than the Tear Dress, as Dr Alice Mackrell observed in *Art and Fashion*. This particular gown was a direct comment on the Spanish Civil War. Inspired by Dali's *Three Young Surrealist Women Holding in Their Arms the Skins of an Orchestra,* the elegant silk crepe dress was festooned with the same disturbing images of death and destruction. Many of Schiaperelli's clients were the wives of foreign dignitaries and inevitably this garment would have made an appearance at state functions and social gatherings of the famous and influential. The fabric and structure of the garment may have epitomised wealth and glamour but it also carried a stark political message.

Following Christian Dior's introduction of the Carolle line in 1947, otherwise known as the New Look, fashionable women began wearing the 'waspie'; a belt-like corset that did not extend more than a few inches above and below the waist. This return to the extreme hourglass figure was greeted with dismay and anger in some circles by those who believed that women had been encased and restricted by their underwear for long enough.

Despite the objections from this rather vocal minority, 1950s women strapped themselves into waspies and girdles with gusto and although the style was once again far removed from their natural form, the new shape symbolised sophistication, glamour and a youthful vitality that had been absent during the humdrum war years. Hollywood paraded the new fashion on the figures of screen goddesses and teenagers wore their narrow waists and wide skirts with bobby socks as they danced to the new sound of rock and roll.

The trussed-up nature of this fashion in underwear was a direct reflection of women's position during the post-war years. Women who had assumed the responsibilities of their menfolk during the war years were dutifully thanked and sent back exactly where they came from – home. Across America, Britain and especially Ireland, a woman's role appeared to be entirely domestic despite what they had achieved only a few years before or how well they had succeeded in their studies.

The consumer boom during the 1950s brought about a surge in advertising most of which featured women excelling at their domestic chores. Home was a woman's rightful domain and the realm in which she could pursue excellence. Success was a happy home with a family to nurture. Advertising revenue soared and domestic duties were presented as an opportunity to prove oneself as a good woman, wife and mother. The restrictive underwear which women once again found themselves wearing was completely in tune with their role as the fashionable domestic chattel.

Chevy or Cadillac?

Not only were women persuaded to shine in their domestic chores, they were also reminded of their conjugal duties and for the first time since the 1910s lingerie was worn both to enhance the figure and to be sexually alluring – women could fulfill the Hollywood dream.

American manufacturer Frederick Mellinger hit upon a bright idea one morning in his Los Angeles office – instead of solely relying upon a team of designers to come up with the new ideas for his latest line in lingerie he would research his market and ask the audience his underwear was designed to impress: men.

In addition to his guarantee of success in the bedroom, Mellinger targeted millions of women all over America and Europe with the promise that they would also be emulating the stars they revered so much. The movie industry's influence upon fashion was still considerable and Mellinger's sexually provocative lingerie promised the hourglass shape most women envied so that they could copy their favourite starlets from the skin up.

Mellinger's marketing strategy was aggressive: he objectified women and portrayed them as possessions to be admired and, more importantly, improved. One particularly famous advertisement alleged that a woman 'walked into Frederick's of Hollywood looking like a Chevy and left looking like a Cadillac'.

Mellinger designed and promoted his underwear line as lingerie to be appreciated by men as much as women. Previously brassieres had been marketed as a woman's secret weapon and a device they could employ to change their shape, enhance their figures and achieve the bust they had always wanted. Mellinger promoted his line of underwear as aspirational: in addition to their shape-enhancing duties they suggested the possibility of something more. He convinced his market that lingerie could help women live out their Hollywood dreams and fulfil the fantasies of their men at the same time and there was nothing secret about it. In other words, Mellinger had hit the jackpot.

Contraception, Controversy and Control

Ireland made the decision to become a member of the European Economic Community in 1961 and, although it was not fully incorporated until 1973, the decision marked the beginning of international economic and cultural influence upon the Republic.

The Catholic Church and the State may have banned contraception but that didn't stop Irish women grasping at the opportunity to finally take charge of their own fertility. A number of doctors and a handful of Family Planning clinics found ways and means of prescribing the revolutionary pill to thousands of women eager to prevent becoming pregnant and to exert control over the size of their families.

Irish national television also began broadcasting on New Year's Eve of 1961 and proved to be an important medium for discussion on the subject of women and their social and cultural position.

Luke Gibbons recorded in 'From Kitchen Sink to Soap; Drama and the Serial Form in Irish Television' that a specially-convened conference on the challenge of Irish national broadcasting called for indigenous programmes on married life:

> A feminine ideal is a necessity for young girls and the absence of any regular 'heroines' on television screens was stated to be injurious to young girls, particularly teenagers. Serial features on women heroines such as Elizabeth Fry, Edel Quinn, the Angel of Dien Bien Phu, or some of the valiant women of the Old Testament could be attractively presented and should contain enough drama to satisfy even male as well as female viewers.

Although RTÉ (Radio Telefís Éireann) was charged with making programmes that celebrated the family and traditional values it also became an important platform for the Women's Liberation Movement. The live discussion programmes broadcast on radio and television became an invaluable forum for public debate and the dissemination of information.

Traditionally developments in western culture had been slow to impact upon Ireland but during the 1960s and 1970s this gradually began to change. Fashion was perhaps the most accessible form of expression for young Irish men and women whose political and social lives were still very much dominated by the Church and State.

Hemlines began to rise, exposing inches of thighs on the streets of Irish cities and towns, thus consigning the hip-length girdle to the back of the wardrobe. The American style of pantihose became popular as mini-skirts simply could not be worn with cumbersome stockings and suspenders. High street shops and department stores had begun commissioning their own lines of lingerie and hosiery so such changes in underwear fashions were no longer just to be read about in the pages of magazines.

The mini-skirt and the boyish figures associated with much of 1960s fashions marked a significant change in an industry that had previously been directed towards grown women as opposed to teenagers. The 1960s were unabashed in dismissing the sophisticated elegance that had dominated womenswear for previous decades. Fashion was deliberately distancing itself from the stuffy ateliers of Paris and had moved down to explore the hustle and bustle of the street.

Wealthy heiress Edie Sedgwick embodied this exuberant rejection of the past in her role as muse for pop artist Andy Warhol. A high society east coast It-girl, Sedgwick arrived on the New York scene having run away from Harvard wearing little else apart from her grandmother's jewellery. She quickly hooked up with Warhol and his hedonistic cohorts and set up camp in his Manhattan nightclub, The Factory. She dyed her hair ashen-grey to match Warhol's silvery mop and often dressed in nothing more than black tights and a leotard. In 1965 her unique style prompted *Life* magazine to record her as:

This crop-mop girl with the eloquent legs is doing more for black tights than anybody since Hamlet.

Although Sedgwick's wealthy father provided the necessary funds for her social life and shopping trips, her style (often a result of collaboration with Warhol) was directional. She would arrive at parties barefoot and wearing nothing but a mink coat and oversized earrings. Sedgwick's style not only influenced her contemporaries but was also a source of inspiration for fashion houses such as Christian Dior, which has since reinvented her iconic look on more than one occasion.

Sedgwick's alabaster skin and elfin physique typified the 1960s boyish look which was far removed from the curved hips and pointed bosoms of the previous decade. Although women had been liberated from tiny waists, the overall effect was more childlike than androgynous. Set in the context of the significant developments taking place within the women's movement across the United States and Europe, these fashions seem like a form of appeasement to a society unnerved by their advancement.

> " **Nature may be against Irish women. May? What an understatement!** "

Women's issues may have become the subjects of public debate but in Ireland, very little had changed. Contraception may have been available for the determined, and foreign popular culture had made its mark on the fashion sensibilities of the young, but the foundations of society remained the same.

In a 1963 edition of Irish magazine, *Woman's Way*, the editor, Ed O'Sullivan, compared the plight of Irish women to that of the 'Negroes in Mississippi'. In between advertisements for engagement rings, bridal dresses and diet plans, he observed that nature was against all women and contended that they had never been taken seriously by western society:

> Trouble with women may be the same trouble with the Negroes in Mississippi and South Africa, and the 'greens' in the northern precincts of this little island – they've just never been taken seriously and given the chances ...
>
> ... Nature may be against women. May? What an understatement! As long as humans are designed the way they are, I think women will have to remain being underprivileged and unequal. Democracy and the western way of life, no less than dictatorship and the eastern way of life, are against women, just as are the law of the jungle and the survival of the fittest.

A large proportion of 1960s fashion was in fact a reinvention of the 1920s – a period which also brought significant change for women in Ireland and much of Europe. Within years of putting their stamp on the ballot paper their most fashionable garments bore more resemblance to the clothes worn by their younger brothers than their mothers. Four decades and a second wave of feminist activism later and women were once again dressed like children; the only difference being this time round they were not expected to rely on girdles and 'roll-ons'. Instead of squeezing their figures into narrow clothing, women began slimming their bodies by dieting. It was no longer satisfactory for underwear to manipulate and coerce the body, fashion and society began demanding women permanently reduce their size from within.

Bras and the Battle of the Sexes

By the 1970s, the Battle of the Sexes had begun in earnest. Kate Millett's *Sexual Politics* riled the American writer and commentator Norman Mailer so much that he suggested 'women should be kept in cages'. Germaine Greer had challenged all self-professed emancipated women to savour their own menstrual blood and described a woman's chest as a millstone around her neck in her 1971 polemic, *The Female Eunuch*:

> *It endears her to the men who want to make their mammet of her, but she is never allowed to think that their popping eyes actually see her. Her breasts are only to be admired for as long as they show no signs of their function: once darkened, stretched or withered they are objects of revulsion ...*

Greer called upon women to discard their bras and maintained they were the very garments responsible for perpetuating the myth of the rounded, pert bosom. Greer believed the only way women could escape the tyranny of the chest was if society came to accept the natural, free-hanging breast. Greer's writing was radical and her outspoken manner and anarchist determination to upturn social constructs surrounding women's dress, appearance, social position and behaviour changed the perspective of men and women all over the world

For decades the only aspect of her body a woman could control was her shape. Now feminist activists urged women to demand a different kind of control: independence. Women across Europe and the United States began protesting for equal pay, legal protection from domestic violence and improved access to contraception.

In Ireland the debate was particularly high profile and raged over the airwaves and across the pages of newspapers and magazines. In a 1971 edition of *Woman's Way* magazine, many readers' letters featured queries relating to contraception and pregnancy. One eighteen-year-old girl wrote that she had become pregnant by a married man with three children. She explained that he refused to leave his family and she asked the 'Agony Aunt' whether or not she should travel to England. The implication here was that once in England she would have a termination, a procedure that was and remains illegal in Ireland. Her query received a curt response:

> Contact the Catholic Protection and Rescue Society, 30 South Anne Street, Dublin 2. Indeed you should not go to England, for you can get all the help you need here.

A few weeks later however, the publication featured an extended article on contraception and family planning that took a rather different line. The writer interviewed a number of doctors and counsellors working in the field of family-planning who were very frank about the safest methods of contraception. Dr Anne Legge from the Fertility Guidance Clinic on Merrion Square, Dublin, is quoted as saying:

> The Rhythm and Thermometer methods are the most unreliable ones there are, so they are not recommended at the clinic. If the Pill is not suitable for a woman, she will probably be fitted for an internally worn diaphragm, which she must insert with a special cream before intercourse. Alternatively she might be advised to go to a hospital in the North to have a small plastic coil inserted in her womb. Both these devices must be bought in the six counties or in England, as their sale is still prohibited in the Republic.

The same edition of the magazine also featured interviews with various representatives of the Catholic Church who denigrated the very notion of contraception. Unlike the previous article, they waxed lyrical about the sacrament of marriage and the reliable methods in which a woman could monitor her own fertility with nothing more than a thermometer and a calendar!

Woman's Way magazine had left no stone uncovered as while providing information on contraception and how to get access to it they had also satisfied the readers who held more conservative views. This informed middle-ground epitomised Irish morality; on one hand the editorial reminded readers of the laws of the Church and State and on the other it quite frankly detailed how to go about bending them.

In between these articles ran an advertisement for Triumph's lycra pantie-girdle: 'The Doreen Double'. The accompanying image featured a woman's body from chest to thigh, wearing the rather substantial 'Doreen', which was described as 'strong and light' with a special lace trim 'that won't slow circulation as some too-tight elastic does'. The notion that adequate blood supply is an added bonus is quite illuminating, particularly when it accompanies an illustration of a headless – and therefore brainless – female body. Nevertheless, underewear was an essential item of every woman's wardrobe. Greer's suggestion of abandoning the bra does not come with an alternative and although her suggestion that women go through life with their breasts unsupported might have been fine advice for someone mentally equipped to take on Norman Mailer, it wasn't much good for the 1960s woman who just wanted control over her own fertility.

During this period, Greer was one of numerous outspoken feminist voices which demanded that woman cast off their bras. Although most women did not, primarily because they practically could not, fashionable underwear had become less obtrusive and more subtle. The heavy stitching and wiring had been replaced by soft cottons and less structured design.

Inevitably, this style did not suit the requirements of all women and by the mid 1970s underwear designer Janet Reger had attracted an international following by specifically catering for women who preferred more elaborate lingerie. Her infamy even stretched to London's West End as a character in a Tom Stoppard play exclaimed, 'Don't get your Janet Regers in a twist'.

Janet Reger had cornered the market in seductive lingerie during a period when the high street offered little more than big pants or 'barely-there' underwear. Reger first opened in the mid-1960s promising women they could be 'Marilyn Monroe by night and feel a million dollars every day' which was in fact very close to the truth as a Janet Reger negligee was priced at around £950 stg. Her diaphanous lace bras and satin knickers were in stark contrast to the stiff, whirlpool-stitched bras and the more fashionable flimsy cottons of the period. Reger designed her lingerie with one thing in mind – sex.

By the mid 1970s, Janet Reger had established a multi-million pound business. Her designs were worn by Hollywood stars and royalty and she reportedly received a steady stream of letters from grateful husbands and wives thanking her for reviving their fading sex lives.

Underwear as Outerwear

As women started to make an impression in the boardroom they began to feel as though they needed to make an even bigger impact in the bedroom. Sex had become the advertising world's most reliable tool, selling everything from shaving foam to beer. In previous decades it was a woman's face and figure which dictated her level of appeal but once women had started to exert pressure in business, it became necessary to assert their sexual identity right down to their underpants. Whether this was a reminder to themselves or a bid to comfort the men around them is uncertain.

Underwear had become 'lingerie' and it was no longer playing a supporting role as once the tailored armour had come off, the 1980s working woman was dressed for something rather different. The more visible women's impact upon the workplace became, the greater seemed society's desire to strip them naked, a pattern that is still evident today.

It was around this time that the thong started to gain popularity among young women in particular. Otherwise known as the 'G-string' or just plain 'string', the thong was initially considered to be an overtly sexual item of lingerie and typified the 1980s working woman's determination to succeed in both the boardroom and the bedroom. Interestingly, the thong is reminiscent of the style of clothing previously worn by Native American males and although a black lace thong is a far cry from the hide of a North American water buffalo, the 1980s woman was also a hunter-gatherer of sorts and there is no doubt she needed to be prepared for battle.

In recent years the thong has become mainstream largely due to the fashion for ever more close-fitting clothing and the aversion to showing the outline of underwear.

Nowadays the thong is not considered quite so provocative and has taken on a more functional role, often constructed from very sheer fabric to ensure it keeps a low profile.

No sooner had Madonna decided she was a 'Boy Toy' (she wore a belt buckle adorned with this label on several occasions at the beginning of her career) than millions of young women all over the world empowered by her trend-setting style began copying her trademark look of exposed bra straps and translucent lace tops. Underwear had become outerwear and there was no turning back.

When it comes to the contents of our underwear drawers, Madonna has a lot to answer for. As someone who has earned a reputation both as a trend-setter and a vigorous trend-follower, the careful construction of her image is a popular cultural reference point. Madonna's infamous corsets have had their impact on lingerie departments all over the world and although she is not the first nor will be the last to resurrect them, she is perhaps the most famous.

Madonna chose to wear her most protective clothing at one of the most successful points of her career: the Blonde Ambition tour in 1989. As part of her stage costume she wore two Jean-Paul Gaultier basques. The first was in dusky pink with pointed breasts and was initially worn underneath a pinstripe, double-breasted trouser suit that was slashed on either side of the chest to ensure the pink points of the breast were peeking through. The second corset in gold was worn during the most controversial section of the show where she simulated masturbation to the tune of one of her earliest hits, 'Like A Virgin'.

Madonna has often found new ways of manipulating her image to attract attention from the broader public audience and her impact and ability to provoke debate has never been confined simply to those who buy her music. The difference between Madonna's reasoning and that of the women who sculpted their bodies with whalebone one hundred years earlier, is that Madonna's bustier acted both as a protective shield and a showcase for her strong, muscular body, while the corsetry of her ancestors' generation was a form of physical control. Her carefully choreographed persona and chameleon-like image has ensured constant media attention so it is hardly surprising she opts for underwear associated with empowerment. There is no doubt Madonna's bustier permitted freedom of movement as evidenced by her energetic dance routines and although she too was influenced by fashion, unlike the women of previous decades, she wore her shape-enhancing underwear on the outside. No longer a secret, no longer a mystery, but a very clear statement of power.

Furthermore, she also subverted notions that a corset could restrain a woman's sexuality as her gold basque seemed only to enhance hers when she created a furore over her onstage simulation of masturbation. Instead of being controlled, Madonna and her basque controlled and manipulated the media and, by consequence, public opinion. Madonna had created yet another image of herself; no longer a 'Boy Toy' she was a 'taboo-breaking' and uncompromising artist.

Towards the end of the twentieth century, as women began to exert more control over their own lives and those of others, their underwear became more shape-defining. One designer who deliberately stayed outside of this trend was Calvin Klein.

Klein's range of underwear, characterised by its soft, unstructured design, has proved extremely popular but more so for the brand he has created than the product. His use of directional models like Kate Moss and various movie stars to promote his line of clothing says more about the lifestyle he wanted his clothes to create than the actual garments themselves. The images of Moss' fragile, almost childlike body, wearing only Calvin Klein briefs, draped around the muscular physique of rap artist Marky Mark went beyond an advertisement for underwear. Moss was a relative in-genue in the world of modelling, still a teenager, with a fresh-faced, undiluted beauty. She embodied the Klein brand of unspoilt youth and style.

Girl Power

Writing in *The Beauty Myth*, first published in 1990, Naomi Wolf explored her belief that women seek their idols from the movie screen and pages of magazines, due to what she considered to be a dearth of accessible female role models. She suggested that culture could not accept women as both beautiful and intelligent. She listed a number of literary references to back up her case such as Leah and Rachel in *The Old Testament*, Mary and Martha in the *New*, Hermia and Hermione in *A Midsummer Night's Dream*, Glinda and the Wicked Witch of the West in *The Wizard of Oz*. All good examples but what about Jane Eyre and Emma Woodhouse, not to mention Wonder Woman, Lois Lane and Nancy Drew?

Twentieth-century female role models don't fit quite so easily into boxes and as the millennium drew closer one group of young women took the world by storm. The Spice Girls, a manufactured girl group, rose to fame in 1996 when their first single 'Wannabe' entered the charts at No.1. Hollering their mantra of 'Girl Power' at every opportunity they became one of the most successful pop groups in history and a marketing phenomenon. The winning cocktail of five girls, each with a nickname in accordance with their public persona, created a breadth of appeal that ensured the Spice Girl brand could sell everything from dolls to breakfast cereals.

Appearances of the Spice Girls were usually dominated by shouting and hysterical laughter. They embodied down-to-earth respectability but despite their cleancut image they were perpetually at odds with themselves. One member of the group, nicknamed 'Baby' Spice, was invariably dressed in dolly-like dresses with her hair in pig-tails and yet her provocative stance was perceived as sexually attractive. She appeared as a grown-up baby-girl, all sexed up and sucking on a lollipop.

Similarly, at the 1997 Brit Awards, Geri Halliwell, otherwise known as 'Ginger Spice', appeared on stage wearing a basque emblazoned with a Union Jack. During the course of her performance the basque slipped revealing her nipple. The incident was widely reported at the time and has since been synonymous with both Halliwell and the Spice Girls generally. Halliwell, one of the most vocal members of the group, wore the basque as a fashion statement in tune with the wave of 'Cool Brittania' prevalent at the time. However, her 'Girl Power' mantra and the success of the Spice Girls, all wrapped up in her sturdy basque, combined with the variable of her wayward nipple, illustrates the contradictory position they occupied.

As the century drew to a close it was clear the corset had made a comeback and just like one hundred years before, fashion was responsible. This time however, the corset had gained some additional responsibilities. It was the modern day woman who laced her own stays – or in actual fact, pulled up her own zipper. It was no longer a restrictive garment of clothing and, most importantly, it was worn for public display; it had become a symbol of strength, protection and power.

Twenty-first Century Woman

Does the twenty-first century woman look at her underwear and see a reflection of herself and the position she occupies in society? Most likely not, first thing in the morning at any rate, but if she should take the notion, careful scrutiny of her drawers might be quite enlightening.

Unlike our ancestors, women of today have a greater degree of choice to wear what suits them and to be who they want. One day might require body-shaping pants and seamless bra while the same evening might be a night for a black lace thong and no bra at all. Perhaps this is the dilemma for the modern woman: she can be vamp, mother and career woman. She can do any of these but can she do all three at once?

Marks and Spencer, described by English daily newspaper, *The Daily Telegraph*, in 1988 as 'the guardians of the nations' nether regions', designed a recent advertisement campaign around this very idea. As part of a promotion featured in *Marie Claire* magazine the advert featured a multiple-choice questionnaire under the headline, 'What lingerie mood are you in today?' The text preceding the quiz reminded the reader that 'she can never have too much underwear – why not invest in a set to reflect every dimension of your personality?' The reader is then invited to use the attached quiz 'to find out what kind of girl you are today ...'

Popular culture has become obsessed with categorising women. Women were once segregated on the basis of marriage, followed by career, but in recent years the whole host of categories has mushroomed in an effort to box off the modern day woman. It's almost as if contemporary society isn't quite sure what to do with the woman their mothers' generation has produced.

Magazines and newspapers have changed their tack somewhat in recent years. Where they once pontificated on how women should and could have it all, i.e. career, family, beauty and an earth-shattering sex life, they now devote the same column inches to scare-mongering articles on declining fertility and the latest 'must-have' cosmetic surgery. The same space that was once devoted to encouraging women to get out and fend for themselves is now dedicated to reminding women of the tick-tock of their biological clocks in between real-life accounts of career women who have abandoned the boardroom for 24-hour breast feeding, organic vegetables and mother and baby yoga classes.

Instead of celebrating their independence (as popular culture has done with the bachelor since time began) the single woman has been demonised, pitied, laughed at and generally made to appear ridiculous. The best example of this is Bridget Jones; the thirty-something character created by author Helen Fielding and immortalised by Hollywood actress Renée Zellweger.

Bridget is a single woman, frustrated by her stalemate career, dissatisfied with the home she has made for herself, unhappy with her weight and perpetually upbraiding herself for the few pleasures she allows herself such as smoking, chocolate croissants and a few too many shots of vodka.

As a twenty-first century single woman Bridget doesn't fit into any of the camps constructed for her, she is neither successful career woman nor mother, she is not stunningly beautiful nor skin-crawlingly ugly. The reality of her life is perpetually at odds with her ideal and on one occasion, when dressing for a night of potential passion, she opts for 'tummy control' knickers instead of seductive, satin panties in the belief the shape-enhancing qualities of the former are more likely to induce the occasion the latter is intended for. In the end she gets Mr Right of course and is no longer a square peg in a round hole but she never stops being plagued with self-doubt, a characteristic which the audience is expected to find endearing.

The range of underwear available is so expansive it is often daunting and this is despite the best efforts of retailers to present lingerie as a garment that will provide understanding and reassurance.

In May 2000, Germaine Greer wrote an article for the British newspaper, *The Guardian*, on the subject of underwear. Under the headline 'Knickers – Who needs 'em?' she reiterated her opinion that bras contort breasts into a shape far removed from their natural state. Throughout the article she repeats that she opts not to wear knickers or bras for reasons of comfort, in addition to refusing to conform to society's expectations of shape and body control.

Her 1970s war cry which encouraged women to cast aside their bras because they were symbolic of a patriarchal society is transformed into a more practical reasoning that such items of underclothes are simply uncomfortable. This is not to say that her views have altered dramatically but her change of delivery illustrates how she perceives society has changed.

> It was a part of my feminist battle against pornography that I would not tackle up. A century ago randy little boys would pore over the corsetry advertisements in women's magazines and as the pornography industry has grown up it has elaborated this voyeuristic fixation. The passivity and vulnerability of the female subject of male erotic interest is accentuated by her being captured, as it were, as she undresses ... Corsets are uncomfortable; lace is supremely uncomfortable; suspender belts are ridiculous; most brassieres fake rather than control the

bosom. There are men who secretly yearn to wear all this kit. We may ask even of the men who do not, is it us they love or these fetishistic garments?

Her message is just as strong as it was thirty years ago, if not more sinister because not only does she believe that underwear perpetuates a myth of the female image but that it is also the tool of the voyeuristic pornographer. Despite her stern view, Greer does not rally her reader to dress as she does, but instead writes about her own feelings and opinions and frankly tells of the disappointment expressed by her 'Italian lover' when he discovers her bra-less bosom beneath her clothes.

But, as statistics in lingerie sales continue to indicate, Greer's perspective is not one that is shared by the majority of women. There are many styles of underwear and it is not all the costume of porn stars. Women continue to buy, receive and wear underwear because they like it.

The notion that a woman purchases a bra because she feels that by wearing it she will be transformed into society's vision of the physical 'ideal' is ludicrous. Bra-buying women should be given more credit. In today's society where women are expected to excel at home and at work it is no accident that lingerie is promoted as a second skin. Bras and pants are festooned with labels promising to 'mould', 'support' and 'push-up'. After the political leaps and bounds made by women during the last one hundred years, the pressure is on to succeed and our underwear seems to be providing the support.

Epilogue

A woman and her underwear has always been and continues to be, a complicated affair.

Throughout all the twists and turns of fashion and figures, politics and policy, underwear was and remains a reflection of women and the society they inhabit. Fashion in underwear may have changed dramatically but one aspect of the relationship remains constant: a woman needs her underwear.

Underclothes were once the all-important foundation layer of an outfit without which a woman simply could not get dressed. Contemporary underwear may not manipulate shape so dramatically but it still plays an important role in a woman's wardrobe. It is no longer expected to coerce the body into the ideal shape because the ultimate physique is beyond the bounds of possibility for most women. The tyranny of body shaping has shifted from being the charge of underwear to the wearer herself. Today's lingerie provides structure and support of a psychological and emotional nature.

Some women feel they must wear their underwear to conceal while others wear it to exhibit. A woman often places as much emphasis on her bridal trousseau as her wedding dress. For some, underwear provides more comfort than any other item of clothing. Lingerie can be soft and endearing or erotic and domineering.

But in the end, the style, purpose and effect is all dependent upon the woman herself. Lingerie is the first thing a woman puts on and the last she, or someone else, removes. If you want to know a woman, cast your eye over her underwear.

Acknowledgements

I would like to thank:

The National Library of Ireland
The Ulster Museum in Belfast
The Victoria and Albert Museum in London

My friends and colleagues in *The Sunday Tribune* newspaper without whom this book would never have seen the light of day.

My friends at home and away for their support and encouragement over late night phonecalls and long lunches.

Finally, I would like to thank my parents, my brother Andrew and my sister Jennifer.

Further Reading

Breward, Christopher. *Fashion* (Oxford University Press, 2003)

Clear, Caitriona. *Women of the House: Women's Household Work in Ireland 1922–1961* (Irish Academic Press, 2000)

Cox, Caroline. *Lingerie, A Lexicon of Style* (Scripton Editions, 2000)

Cullen Owens, Rosemary. 'Votes for Women', *Labour History News*, Summer 1993.

de la Haye, Amy, and Tobin, Shelley. *Chanel, The Couturière at Work* (The Victoria and Albert Museum, 2003)

Derrick, Robin, and Muir, Robin, *Unseen Vogue, The Secret History of Fashion Photography* (Little, Brown and Company, 2002)

Edgeworth, Maria. *Literary Letters for Ladies* (Everyman, 1993)

Engelmeier, Peter W. and Regine. *Fashion in Film* (Prestel, 1997)

Farrell, Brian, ed. *De Valera's Constitution and Ours*. (Dublin, 1988)

Galligan, Yvonne. *Women and Politics in Contemporary Ireland* (Pinter, 1998)

Gibbons, Luke. 'From Kitchen Sink to Soap; Drama and the Serial Form in Irish Television' in McLoone, Martin and MacMahon, John, eds. *Television and Irish Society* (Dublin, 1984)

Gillespie, Elgy, ed. *Changing the Times, Irish Women Journalists 1965–1981* (The Lilliput Press, 2003)

Greer, Germaine. *The Female Eunuch* (Paladir, 1971)

Greer, Germaine. *The Whole Woman* (Doubleday, 1999)

Gurley Brown, Helen. *Sex and the Single Girl* (Barricade Books, 1962)

Harry Brown, Peter, and Broeske, Pat H. *Howard Hughes, The Untold Story* (Time Warner, 1996)

Hawthorne, Rosemary. *Bras, A Private View* (Souvenir Press, 1992)

Hayes, Alan, and Urquart, Diane. *The Irish Women's History Reader* (Routledge, 2001)

Hill, Maureen. *Women in the Twentieth Century* (Chapman Publishers, 1991)

Lurie, Alison. *The Language of Clothes* (Henry Holt, 1981)

Mackrell, Alice. *Art and Fashion* (Batsford, 2005)

Morgan, Austen, and Purdie, Bob, ed. *Ireland: Divided Nation, Divided Class* (London, 1980)

Parkes, Susan M., ed. *A Danger to the Men? A History of Women in Trinity College Dublin 1904–2004* (The Lilliput Press, 2004)

Robinson, Julian. *The Fine Art of Fashion, An Illustrated History* (Bay Books, n.d)

Steele, Valerie. *The Corset, A Cultural History* (Yale University Press, 2001)

Taylor, Emma, and Sharkey, Lorelei. *Nerve's Guide to Sex Etiquette* (Hodder, 2004)

The Phaidon Fashion Book (Phaidon, 1998)

Tomczak, Sarah, and Pask, Rachel. *Panties; A Brief History* (Dorling Kindersley, 2004)

Vreeland, Diana, *with* Hemphill, Christopher. *Allure* (Little, Brown and Company, 2002)

Willett, C., and Cunnington, Phillis. *The History of Underclothes* (Dover Publications, 1992)

Wolf, Naomi. *The Beauty Myth* (Vintage, 1991)